ADVERSITY

Poetry on the theme of adversity, from poets around the world.

Vol.2

THE POET
Autumn 2021

Compiled by Robin Barratt

THE POET

A leading international online poetry magazine, recognized for both its quarterly themed collections, and its interviews with poets worldwide; looking at their work and their words, and what motivates and inspires them to write.

Interviews, profiles, articles, quarterly collections, Poet of the Week, Poetry Courses and Young Poets.

www.ThePoetMagazine.org

~

ADVERSITY
Vol.2

Published by THE POET

ISBN: 9798496718929

© THE POET, October 2021, and all the authors herein

E: Robin@ThePoetMagazine.org

Cover image and design: Canva
www.Canva.com

Compiled and published for THE POET by:
Robin Barratt Publishing
Affordable Publishing Services

www.RobinBarratt.co.uk

THE POET is sponsored by:

If you would also like to sponsor THE POET, please go to:

www.thepoetmagazine.org/support-us

THANK YOU!

THANK YOU TO EVERYONE, EVERYWHERE SUPPORTING THE POET; WITHOUT YOUR HELP WE WOULDN'T BE ABLE TO CONTINUE SHOWCASING INSPIRING POETS AND PUBLISHING AMAZING POETRY ...

... AND WHAT A DULL WORLD THAT WOULD BE!

WE NEED YOUR SUPPORT!

Love poetry? Then please support or sponsor us too; everything goes back into showcasing poets and promoting poetry from around the world.

Go to the website for further details:

www.ThePoetMagazine.org

CONTENTS

141. Nivedita Karthik - INDIA
145. Kakoli Ghosh - INDIA
149. Bill Cushing - CALIFORNIA, USA
153. Rachel Elion Baird - MASSACHUSETTS, USA
157. Brajesh Singh - INDIA
161. Kate Young - ENGLAND
165. Bill Cox - SCOTLAND
167. Vesna Mundishevska-Veljanovska - REPUBLIC OF NORTH MACEDONIA
169. Gabriella Garofalo - ITALY
173. Tracy Davidson - ENGLAND
177. Cheryl-lya Broadfoot - ENGLAND
181. Shaswata Gangopadhyay - INDIA
183. Jill Sharon Kimmelman - DELAWARE, USA
185. Jane Fuller - SCOTLAND
189. Ian Cognitō - CANADA
193. Adrienne Stevenson - CANADA
197. Anamika Nandy - INDIA
199. Wilda Morris - ILLINOIS, USA
203. Kathleen Bleakley - AUSTRALIA
205. John Laue - CALIFORNIA, USA
209. Vernes Subašić - BOSNIA AND HERZEGOVINA
213. Paula Bonnell - MASSACHUSETTS, USA
215. Madhavi Tiwary - KINGDOM OF BAHRAIN / INDIA
217. Ankita Patel - INDIA
219. Janet Bi Li Chan - AUSTRALIA
223. Carol Casey - CANADA
227. Rose Menyon Heflin - WISCONSIN, USA
231. Prafull Shiledar - INDIA
235. Lisa Molina - TEXAS, USA
237. Aaron Pamei - INDIA
239. Monica Manolachi - ROMANIA
241. Maid Čorbić - BOSNIA AND HERZEGOVINA
243. Alun Robert - ENGLAND
247. Suchismita Ghoshal - INDIA
251. Dr. Achingliu Kamei - INDIA
255. Julie Ann Tabigne - SINGAPORE / PHILIPPINES
257. Mary Anne Zammit - MALTA
259. Jenelyn Leyble - SINGAPORE / PHILIPPINES
261. Hanh Chau - CALIFORNIA, USA
263. Maria Editha Turingan Garma-Respicio - HONG KONG / PHILIPPINES

ADVERSITY
noun

adverse or unfavourable fortune or fate; a condition marked by misfortune, calamity, or distress:
Friends will show their true colours in times of adversity.

an adverse or unfortunate event or circumstance:
You will meet many adversities in life.

www.Dictionary.com

Rhonda Parsons
ILLINOIS, USA

Rhonda discovered she had a talent for writing when she elected to take creative writing at Hononegah High School. Since then, she has received an award from Rock Valley College and the Rockford Writers' Guild, for her book *If A Picture Is Worth A Thousand Words*. She is currently working on another collection of poems called *Take 5*. She's also shared her vision in newspaper editorials, and performed publicly at Holy Day celebrations.

E: lilyspanda7@yahoo.com

MUSCLE MEMORY

Kindle the fire of love
burn away the veils
Does my heart have muscle memory
to tread this winding path?

It's more uphill, than down
walking into wind and rain
forests deep and green.

Sometimes, there's nary a bird
no light on the forest floor

My hearts walked on through it all
past the pain, the boredom.

I've been called the Devil
slapped by twigs,
wild brush.

I lit a match. Set fire to their limbs
gave my heart a warm, soft glow

Tell me heart, is this muscle memory?

Be anxiously concerned with the needs of the world
love the light, not the lamp
empty myself, be hollow as a reed

Does my heart have muscle memory
to complete this noble quest?
I can feel my soul pick up a guitar
sing by the warm fire
it's a campfire song
but it sounds like the Heavenly Concourse

it stirs me when I'm wasting time,
dwelling on earthly things

in those moments my soul gets wings
flies to another realm

I ask them to sing over and over

they always acknowledge my request
away, I fly
and when I return
I'm ready to illumine the world.

Why does my heart ponder about its capacity;
its muscle memory to be?
It knows how to use words
to make the soul think,
make it cry, in a healing way

I used to like my 3x5's crisp, no creases in the cover
my books pristine, margins clear
 only highlights of yellow colour

But, paper Is the Penholder's heart
and words are the arteries
they have one desire,
to give life to the reader
so, it needs attention and care
Those creases say it's been walked, been hugged,
and the arteries are carrying good blood.

Those yellow marks
highlight the oxygen,
the Spirit I gleaned from within
Therefore, I say
"let's mark up the margins,
show my search for the Spirit within."

Sugar cookies with the taste of coconut oil
I'd thought I'd miss them too
But after encountering a world
politicizing a virus, spitting out science,
limiting pro-life to a fetus
surely the spiritual worlds serve sweeter food!

But I'm still here
My heart walks on through the wind and rain
uphill, long and winding
through the wilderness
despite its blisters, scratches
or perhaps, Because of them
my heart has a song
in tune with Mother Earth

it goes something like this
love dub, love dub, love dub

Does my heart have muscle memory?
I have no doubt!

Andrea Carter Brown
CALIFORNIA, USA

Andrea is the author of *September 12*, published by The Word Works for the 20th anniversary of 9/11. Her three previous poetry collections are *Domestic Karma* (Finishing Line Press, 2018), *The Disheveled Bed* (CavanKerry Press, 2006), and *Brook & Rainbow* (winner of the Sow's Ear Press Chapbook Prize, 2001). *American Fraktur*, her current manuscript, won the 2018 Rochelle Ratner Memorial Award from Marsh Hawk Press. Her poems have won awards from Five Points, River Styx, The MacGuffin, and the Poetry Society of America, among others, and are cited in the Library of Congress Online Guide to the Poetry of 9/11. They have been featured on *NPR, Poetry Daily*, and have also appeared in *Ploughshares, The Gettysburg Review, Mississippi Review*, and *Southwest Review*. She was a Founding Editor of *Barrow Street* and Managing Editor of The *Emily Dickinson Journal*. For six years, she served on the Virginia Center for the Arts (VCCA) Fellows Council, the last three as Chair, where she edited the poetry anthology *Entering the Real World: VCCA Poets on Mt. San Angelo*, for VCCA's 40th anniversary with Margaret B. Ingraham. Since 2017 she has been Series Editor of *The Word Works Washington Prize*.
E: waterrail@me.com
W: www.andreacarterbrown.com.
FB: @Andrea Carter Brown
Instagram: #andreabrownpoet
Twitter: @AndreaBrownPoet

THE GARDEN OF EARTHLY DELIGHTS
Homage to Bosch

To save me, you sat in our apartment
the two days it took a cleaning crew
of five to HEPA vacuum and wet wipe
every single object and surface twice.
Once I started coughing up blood,

you schlepped downtown every week
to retrieve the mail. To get there,
you had to walk through the same
gate in the chain link fence topped
with coiled razor wire where dump

trucks and workers coated with dust
passed through a washing station
before they could exit Ground Zero.
It was you who admitted engineers
to test the air and dust yet again; you

who waited in that stuffy acrid air
for someone to pick up the carpets
rolled up on our living room floor
since the morning of September 11.
Those months doctors banned me

from going within two miles of the site,
you did everything. It took three years
to get the asthma I never had before
under control. Save a depressive spell
the following fall, you were my tower

of strength through it all. Six years later
we thought we were over the hump: we
had moved west; we were beginning
to like our new life. December 21, 2007,
out of the blue, like the planes that flew

into the Twin Towers, bad news: you
have kidney cancer. Advanced. Not
eligible for post-surgery drug trials.
Why? A few tiny nodules in your lung,
too small to reliably remove and biopsy,

might be metastatic. Healthy all your life,
never smoked, how could this be? Not
the chlorine in the drinking water
when you were three. The asbestos
insulation you helped your dad install

as a teenager? No. But when you mention
9/11, the oncologist perks up: exposure
to heavy metals is a known cause. No cure
is known. So here we are, you are, eight
years later, fighting now for your life.

First published in *September 12,* (The Word Works, 2021).

AFTER THE MOST RECENT TERRORIST ATTACK
The idea of a house implies belief in a future.

All week, the house next door
is being demolished.

The orange groves that thrived
on limestone

from compressed animal bones
have given way

to acres of faux Spanish houses,
a Valencia

or Navel orange tree in each sunny
front yard.

The elderly couple next door,
Abe and Sallee,

were the first to welcome us.
Frail, but full

of spunk, Abe never tired
of telling

his life story. How many camps had
he survived?

Seven? When neighbours across
the street

enclosed their front yard with a wall
and arched gate,

he complained it reminded him
of Auschwitz,

but refused to say anything to them.
He met Sallee

in Buchenwald. After months in
a displaced persons'

camp, they married, tried chicken
farming

in Southern New Jersey before moving
to this city

with its palm trees and citrus groves.
One day

the house grew quiet. For a year
we lived

dreading the day demolition would
begin.

First published in *September 12,* (The Word Works, 2021).

PEACE

September 11, 2016.

Cross 'George Dickson' with 'Souvenir de Claudius Pernet,'
'Joanna Hill' with 'Charles P. Kilham.' In turn cross their
unnamed seedlings to produce another unnamed seedling,
then cross that with the tea rose 'Margaret McGredy.'

Four years it took a French horticulturalist to hybridize
this new variety, which he named after his mother, 'Mme.
A. Meillard.' By then it was 1939. Foreseeing the invasion
of France, he sent cuttings to Italy, Turkey, Germany,

the United States. The rose survived as 'Gloria Dei.' In
1945, Meillard asked Field Marshall Alan Brooke, whose
D-Day strategy won the war, to give the rose his name.
He suggested 'Peace' instead, the name not official till

the Berlin Wall fell. It doesn't do well in Los Angeles.
Sun too hot, too strong. Forced to move the 'Polka' after
a storm destroyed the wall on which it climbed, we chose
this one to plant in its place. You can love a word so much

you hope a plant so named will live up to it. Years after
your life was uprooted, turned upside-down, you can still
so yearn for peace that you will overlook the fact that you
don't really like anything about this rose except its name.

Hussein Habasch
KURDISTAN / GERMANY

Hussein is a poet from Afrin, Kurdistan. He currently lives in Bonn, Germany. His poems have been translated into English, German, Spanish, French, Chinese, Turkish, Persian, Albanian, Uzbek, Russian, Italian, Bulgarian, Lithuanian, Hungarian, Macedonian, Serbian, Polish and Romanian, and has had his poetry published in a large number of international anthologies. His books include: *Drowning in Roses, Fugitives across Evros River, Higher than Desire and more Delicious than the Gazelle's Flank, Delusions to Salim Barakat, A Flying Angel, No pasarán* (in Spanish), *Copaci Cu Chef* (in Romanian), *Dos Árboles and Tiempos de Guerra* (in Spanish), *Fever of Quince* (in Kurdish), *Peace for Afrin, peace for Kurdistan* (in English and Spanish), *The Red Snow* (in Chinese), *Dead arguing in the corridors* (in Arabic) and *Drunken trees* (in Kurdish). He participated in many international festivals of poetry including: Colombia, Nicaragua, France, Puerto Rico, Mexico, Germany, Romania, Lithuania, Morocco, Ecuador, El Salvador, Kosovo, Macedonia, Costa Rica, Slovenia, China, Taiwan and New York City.
E: habasch70@hotmail.com
FB: @hussein.habasch

THE EMBRACE
Translated by Muna Zinati

When the two lovers heard
The fighter planes roar,
They embraced each other.
When the sound approached more,
They embraced each other more.
When the bombing and destruction began,
They embraced each other tightly.
Now they stand in an embrace in eternity.

O LOVE, O WAR!
Translated by Muna Zinati

O war,
O endless filth,
Leave here, go to hell!
We want to write
Love poems
Without your unpleasant odour penetrating through them.
We want to kiss our wives, sweethearts, and mistresses
Without hearing your noise around us.
We want to die from love, from love alone!

I am in exile, and the war is at its height.
Oh God, how much I missed your small wars, my love,
Your wars in which my heart and I were happy victims.

Go on, be a little crazy, have a little fun;
Or if you want, ruin my mood with your huge dose of grouchiness.
I don't want to think about this nasty war which is taking place in my homeland.

This war is a machine, grinding the meat of love
And crushing its bones with no mercy!
With love, we will grind war's bones and eliminate it!

It seems, this war has no end.
Come, let us plant trees and sleep,
cuddling up next to them until they grow.

Don't say, you have no time.
This war will drag for a long time.
I don't want our love to be defeated.

The lover was saying to his sweetheart,
I will kiss you until dawn.
Now he says,
I will kiss you until this war explodes from rage.

Put your hand on my forehead.
Distract this war that almost crushes my head.
With love, we will crush its head!

War doesn't like to pause,

Doesn't like holidays nor laziness.
It likes work, and it does it with the utmost devotion and dedication;
And the more its work pays off,
The more it grows passionate, energetic, and moves forward.
With love, we will stop it on its track; yes, we will stop it...

War doesn't listen, doesn't obey nor answer to anybody.
It goes to its goal as a fatal bullet goes directly to the heart of life.
We will return the favour twice as hard.

In war,
We won't build a house; we won't put any stone over stone.
We will write poems and sing songs.
Nothing enrages war more than poems and songs.

I will go to war.
"And what will you do there?"
I will kill war!

"What do you do in wartime?"
I write love poems.
"What else?"
I hold on more to love!

Anne Mitchell
CALIFORNIA, USA

For Anne, the year 2020 gifted her solitude, a chance to slow down, observe and focus on her poetry. A year of Wild Writing Circles have been both anchor and flame for thoughts to flourish and become poems. Anne's recent work may be found in the *Community Journal* for writers.
E: annemitchell9@icloud.com

OPEN SESAME

May I walk through this door
from black and white
to meander like Toto in Technicolour,

from the tsunami of trashcans
brimming in discarded winds,
to six inches of sea

on a turquoise atoll,
where birdsong laps fairy houses
gently around my ankles.

May I walk through this door
into a shower of lost valentines,
a downpour of candy hearts into be-mine hands.

May I walk through this door
into the wink of the swan
and float through the tunnel of timelessness.

If the door is locked,
I'll massage it with both palms,
to open sesame with a soft whisper,

or I'll pick the lock with
braided tomorrows, beeswax and bluebonnets,
while singing sonnets to the hinges.

I will walk through this door,
seal it in yesterdays,
picture frames and lost moonbows.

Dr. Sarah Clarke
ENGLAND

Dr. Sarah Clarke lived in the Middle East for 15 years and is the Founder of Baloo's Buddies in Bahrain - a non-profit program using pet dogs to enhance the life and social skills of children with communication difficulties. When not working on large scale inclusive projects, Sarah enjoys writing in a variety of formats including children's literature and poetry. Writing primarily on themes of inclusion, mental health and the environment, Sarah's poems and artwork have been included in a number of international anthologies as well as poetry events and exhibitions in Bahrain.
E: sarah@dscwll.com
FB: @Baloosbuddies
FB: @@sarahclarke888

GONE

A child carried above
Hand to hand
Through desperate crowds
Separated from the life she once had
Up and over the fortress's wall
Pulled into the unknown
By strangers
Last glimpses
Shouts of I love you singed by the stifling air
The ground explodes
Parted forever
Adversity has new meaning

Brian Wake
ENGLAND

Recently a judge at the Wirral Poetry Competition, Brian was born, and currently lives in Liverpool. He has been writing poetry for over forty years, and has had eight books of poems published (Headland Publications). He has also had his work published internationally, and has been broadcast on *BBC 4* and *BBC 2* TV, and on local radio stations around the country.
E: brianwake1@btinternet.com

SIGNS OF SPRING

From Wednesday to Saturday he came and went
In shifts; brought outside in, disguised as flowers,
To her bed. Would take not her but only whiffs
Of disinfected hospital instead back to her garden.
Stones there bled.

A starving dog, he begged for scraps of why and
How just sixteen summers seemed, to her, enough;
So much, in fact, that she should slip upstairs
And try the darkest door.

Clenched fists of hope and questions, he, for four
Days, came on shift around his daughter's bed.
Brought magazines, rolled awkwardly, and folded
Handkerchiefs, and held her hand, and held
The cardboard trays to catch the steaming bile,
And held a cloth to dab the tears. And offered water,
Checking now and then her pulse and that she
Understood how loved she was.

In almost silence, and a half dark ward, with only
Distant footsteps and the pumping instruments
That fought relentlessly against a dozen dying hearts,
He lightly sang to her as much as ever he could sing;
A hundred songs, and softly sung, and watched
Her wintered eyes for signs of spring.

Mónika Tóth

ROMANIA

Mónika graduated high-school in Humanities at Körösi Csoma Sándor in Covasna, and then studied accountancy. She is interested in culture, reading, painting, philosophy and photography, and enjoys Romanian, Turkish, Russian, South-American and Norwegian literature. Her poetry has appeared in Romanian literary magazines such as *Boema* and *Oglinda Literara*, and Hungarian literary magazines *Helikon* and *Napsziget*. Passionate about poetry, her new books *Soványít hiányod* (*Your absence makes me thin*) and *Tu eşti roua dimineții* (You are my early dew) have just been released.
E: monikatoth314@yahoo.com

SOMETIMES PROBLEMS

Sometimes problems appear to come in batches
I lost my mind.
I am sad.
I cry like a child.
That is my life
my dear
I want to smile like you
maybe
I'll survive

Jyoti Nair
INDIA

Jyot's works feature in numerous, global poetry anthologies and journals such as *The Kali Project of Indie Blue Publication, Impspired, Inner Child Press, Open Skies Quarterly, Journal of Expressive Writing,* and *Indian Periodica*l. She has won a number of awards including The Certificate of Excellence by English Poets and Literary Excellence Certificate by Gujarat Sahitya Academy – India.
E: jyotinair2017@gmail.com

WRECKAGES AND WREATHS!

Mornings of my nation have been ire-spitting!
Belabouring our frail vertebrae,
These abominable mornings distil our terror-stricken skies ...
My routinely vivacious mandala sketches whimpering,
In the clutches of famished montages, of alleys and arcades!

Did you say your mercenary-staircase reeks of sodden effluvia?
Prongs of walloping wails, of mothers and fledglings,
Being guzzled by gourmandizing manholes!
Manholes: Bureaucrats sprangling as guileful speech-termites!
Manholes: Pitiful and detestable, can't be methodically closed as part
of rudimentary sanitation!

Cinders of our faith, stirred remorselessly!
Our strangulated prayers, wrestling with demented flocks of sly
viruses ...
Punctuating our air with their menacing shrills, with their ash-
devouring gauntlets!
Abhorrent ciphers stealthily poking our nerve cells,
Don't surmise them as random high-pitched bird songs!

Will our wreaths, be mere waning glimpses of wreckages?
Of innumerable stories and sighs, asphyxiated within the pandemic
chronicles ...
Just to be rummaged perhaps after months, as research-residuum,
for some historical documentaries ...

Jake Aller
SOUTH KOREA / USA

John (Jake) Cosmos Aller grew up in Berkeley, California, and Washington and is a retired U.S. Foreign Service Officer currently living in South Korea. He served in ten countries over a 27-year career with the Department of State. He graduated from the University of Washington with an MPA degree and a MA in Korean studies, and did his undergraduate work at the University of the Pacific in Political Science and Psychology. Before his diplomatic career, John taught ESL, Government, and Asian studies in Korea with the University of Maryland and Kyunghee University. He also served in the Peace Corps in Korea.

E: authorjakecosmosaller@gmail.com
W: www.theworldaccordingtocosmos.com
Twitter: @jakecaller

WILD THINGS

Wild things come out to play
Intending to unleash chaos
Leaving their prisons
Deep inside the mind

The wild things
Have come out to run amok
In the light of the full moon

Nightmarish real foul creatures
Great demons, werewolves, goblins,
Monsters, hell hounds

Escaped banshees
Straight out of Hell
howling at the lunatic
light of the full moon

WILD THINGS RUN AMUCK

4 am
O dark Hundred
bewitching hour
Time for wild things

to escape
from their prisons
deep in the mind
of the sleeping man

they escape
hideous demons
ghouls, goblins, monsters
escaped banshees

the wild things
sniff the air
saying it was time
for some wilding

the wild things
jump out the window
and run amuck
spreading chaos in their wake

killing everyone they see
raping women
vandalizing buildings
yelling screaming

as the wild things
run amuck
Led by a half man half horse
centaur like creature
with a Putin Like mask
and the voice of Donald Trump

the wild things run amuck
all over the town
spreading chaos
until the dawning sun

turns them back
into vampire like creatures
and werewolves
howling at the full moon

the wild things
come back
and enter their prison
deep in the sleeper's head

and the wild things
fade into a nightmarish image
as the sleeping man
awakes recalling the dream

and the night of terror
when the wild things
came out to play
at o dark hundred

Shereen Abraham
UNITED ARAB EMIRATES

A writer, artist, happiness coach, Theta Healer and devotee of all things creative, Shereen believes *'Experience is one of life's best teachers'* and *'Colours are therapeutic'*. For Shereen, it's important that the journey is as exciting as the destination! Over the years she has written several articles and poems that have been published in magazines and anthologies both at home and abroad.
E: shereen.abraham@gmail.com

WHEN THE MASK SLIPPED

You had an alluring reputation that always preceded your name
Charismatic, witty and all things nice being your claim to fame
You certainly lived up to all that and more when we first met
I was delighted as you held my hand and led me into the sunset.
Many beautiful sunsets passed, you made me fall deeply in love with you
I was beside myself and thought how lucky I was to know a love so true
The majestic colours of the sunset whispered promises of a wonderful life
A new day dawned, I felt blissful when we became husband and wife.
Not long after the blissful days, the sunsets lost their magic in my eyes
When at sunset you got home from work, I saw you in disguise
A disguise so terrifying, you turned to one I could barely even recognize
My dreams shattered, my heart ached, I knew my life was no more a paradise.
You in disguise was an antithesis of the one I thought I knew
Leaving me dismayed and horrified at all that you could spew
So shook was I at how my beautiful life quickly blackened
Terrifying, chilling, unreal and eerie, I just felt disheartened.
But the world around us still found you alluring
As you had mastered the art of being charming
Everyone thought you were my greatest blessing
Because no one had a clue of how I was truly feeling.
It was at a grand festive celebration in December
We threw a party at home that all would remember
You were the very charming host dressed to the nines
Regaling everyone with headlines, cuisines and wines.
After dinner, you came to the kitchen looking for me
While I was busy on my own, getting the dessert ready
As was customary you spoke to me quite disrespectfully
I was melancholy, knowing that beneath your mask lurked a bully.
You did not notice our three friends chatting just outside the kitchen
Who were now gaping shocked at what you had so cleverly kept hidden
When you realized your folly, you turned, looked at them and smiled
Wishing you had not let your mask slip, you appeared beguiled.
The party to remember came to an awkward end soon after
The guests left in a hurry pretending like nothing was the matter
Your carefully curated personality was blown to smithereens

You had no clue how to pick up the pieces and not create any scenes.
Who knew the mask would slip one day as you tried to impress
A mask that fit so perfectly it was impossible to guess
How your true self was hidden beneath the many layers
That true self which ever so often reduced me to tears.
But once the mask slipped it became the differentiator
To everyone who thought you were the great charmer
And when they realized that you were actually my tormentor
You were in a quandary as you couldn't keep the charade any longer.

Michal Mahgerefteh
USA / ISRAEL

Michal is an award-winning poet and artist from Israel, living in Virginia, USA, since 1986. She is the author of five poetry chapbooks, two forthcoming in 2022, and is the managing editor of *Poetica Magazine* and *Mizmor Anthology*, and active member of The Poetry Society of Virginia and Voices Israel Poetry Group.
E: mitakart@aol.com
W: www.Mitak-art.com

AND I THOUGHT I WAS GOOD

As I listened deeply, all I heard was
"pre-cancer cells." I stood motionless.
His voice offered warmth and safety,
but mine swallowed the scream.

The news, the kind we feared,
created a historical chasm in my
Book of Life; a savaged flame attempted
to spoil my reality, of today, of tomorrow
O' my cries Mother O' Mother !!!

Suddenly I remembered where I am,
in the *galut, far from those who tailored
my world. Remnants of the past pulsed
traces of hope coloured in shades of olive
and mouth-watering aromas of garlic

and cumin. Distraught, I imagine dark
seraphim and cherubim stumbling down
clay steps as the caress me into Deep Sleep
through the thick swirls of Heavens Gate.
My fears availed this empty dream. Alas!

I paused my breath and muffled, *I can't
do without You and I thought I was good,
wasn't I good? Don't be silent, tell me
I was good am I still so good, so good?*

*Galut - Diaspora

MUTE

grey gravel rocks my car
       as if the earth is rushed apart by an after shock
           "Damn road" I talk to myself
park in front of the back porch
       covered by green algae where carpenter ants
           marching in straight lines
chewing to splinter the wooden rail

I tip toe under a web of jasmine vine
       sniff blooms to calm my adrenaline rush
not looking, I reach for the doorbell
       covered with insect wings woven into silky threads
           warmed to a crisp by rays of midday moon

the side window opens to a sharp screech
           "There you are" vibrates through my earlobe
Ruthie, mother of the bride
       always in a hurry to end conversations. . .
"Come, greet the bride, meet the groom"

hesitant, I say a few mazal tovs
        in words that barely pass my lips
people react impatiently, turn heads with a tight lip
       judges of knowledge in bow ties, snobby PhDs
           mirror each other till boredom

their lack of interest does not need explanation
        I am free, free to forgive, shamelessly forgive
       like Father and Jesus without the Cross
        I feed the seed of my purpose

Shikdar Mohammed Kibriah

BANGLADESH

Shikdar is a globally acclaimed poet, essayist, and short story writer, and has been writing essays on poetry, literature, philosophy, and theology over the last three decades. With an MA in Philosophy, Shikdar is a Principal of an educational institute in his village home in the Sylhet district. His works have always found renowned space in different national and international anthologies, print magazines, e-magazines, and blogs. He is involved in almost 500 literary groups, as well as different newspaper periodic issues around the world. His publications so far include fifteen books: six of poetry, another six on essay, and three short story collections. He is the Founder and President of the popular online group 'Poetry and Literature World Vision.'

E: skibriah@gmail.com

A FUNERAL

I was at a loss when the funeral went on
Surprised at the fleeting time of complex
Equation and can not but upset
At your true dedication to your boss
Nonetheless I opened my rusty windows
To welcome autumnal breeze
At least as a symbolic pose.

I hadn't ever to be experienced
On how the sweat of the farmers
Turn into a suicidal fuel.

Burning paddy! Burning Bangladesh!
An incinerating funeral is going on.

I have a huge experience of bumper crops
Nowadays experience of burning crops.
What a turn of the days changing!

Is it a turn make me back without harvest?
But I know how much you are committed
To your boss all the best.

Stephen Kingsnorth
WALES

Stephen (Cambridge M.A., English & Religious Studies), born in London, retired to Wales from ministry in the Methodist Church with Parkinson's Disease, has had some 300 pieces published by on-line poetry sites, printed journals and anthologies, most recently *Academy of the Heart and Mind, The Parliament Literary Magazine, Runcible Spoon,* and *Poetry Potion.*
E: slkingsnorth@googlemail.com
W: www.poetrykingsnorth.wordpress.com

RELEASE

This prisoner, isolation wing,
wounded, clipped, in stutter nest,
unfettered need, communicate,
beyond the clamp, a grind of teeth,
stumped, just left, ignored, but there.
Light all night, the clock reset,
sidereal, side-tracked from norm,
a clatter plate, enamel slide,
the peep show if a suicide,
to bring him down, cut down to size,
so put in place, box hideaway,
more dust to dust, as when alive.

What device is in my reach
to manipulate, lead by the hand,
if not the shaven head, bone show,
the shrinking flesh, distracted mind?
Perhaps his mother, never known
where son was taken, dead the night,
his debt unknown, collaborate.
Maybe her neighbour, vacant wells,
her son in jail, well-ordered life,
release from shift, except in eyes,
a uniform to wash, dry, press,
from office of the waterboard.

Both sons and mothers, all ignored,
to do, be done by, as are told,
drawn, and quartered, staff block, cell,
blank wall to tell what's scratched on mind.
But can you hear the wailers' songs,
the pitcher's cream, the dripping clock,
through facial cloth, a sodden cough?
Blushed pallor, guilt-edged memories
of those removed from histories,
save stories from their mothers' breasts.

First published by *Sweat and Tears,* August 2021

THE RING CYCLE

Though from next bedroom Wagner crashed
she somehow learned to isolate;
as her table turned on deck
and guitar strumming thrummed through head
she loaned her face to mirror's view
and plucked high brows, her common weal.

Though convex glasses magnify,
her loss ensured repeatedly,
raking feather down from skin
fixtures, fittings gouache mauled.

With open mouth which had sucked thumb
now palette hole, smeared paints above,
the sheen on lids unmatched by cheeks,
maiden stilettos, other lifts,
the girl who played with pogo stick
was now become a clown on stilts.

Her father gone, another come
stepping into prints, spare bed place;
new ring master, of many, first,
attracting through red coat and tales.

SUSPENSE

The thrill of holiday suspends,
at seven age, when trundling train
tracks flimsy girders, river bridge,
at slower speed, for driver knows
his belching monster grinding line
may crack the rails, so carriage fall
with luggage, family and me,
deposit in the muddy swirl,
a fortnight, sediment, to crawl.

The others chatter as before,
the clatter tells they know full well
our destiny - don't scare the boy.
I, wishing back near home turf hedge,
have little care for seaside sand,
the hut below the fall of slopes,
kiddles, mud inter-tidal boat,
still less for journey platform break
awaiting us at Grandma's home.

And then I hear we gain some speed,
soon rhythm over sleepers flies
and suddenly my scenes are back.
The river's gone, the rattles left,
now stony beach, the island mist,
our backs to groynes against the wind,
the Street, the shells, the oyster smells.
The next, the dread of our return,
the chugging through suspended hell.

First published by *Literary Yard*, August, 2020,

Steven Jakobi
USA / HUNGARY

Steven is a native of Budapest, Hungary, but has lived in the United States since 1967. He is a retired college biology professor. His fictional stories and poems have appeared in several publications, and is the author of a book of short essays titled *Birds, Bats, Bugs, Bacteria: Lessons from Nature*.
E: jakobisr@gmail.com
W: www. stevenjakobi.com
FB: @StevenRJakobi
Twitter: @StevenRJakobi
Amazon's author page: Dr. Steven R. Jakob

SITTIN' ON THE STEPS

When you came home
from the city
scared
confused
crying,
I offered you
the only thing
I could give you.
And sat with you
on the front porch
steps and held
your hand
in silence.

SOMEWHERE, SOMEONE

She was born ugly.
No other way to say it.
Especially so,
as her sisters
were pretty.
She grew up ugly.

In school she was
shunned. Adults
turned their heads.
She was alone,
invisible,
an outcast.

She understood the
cruelty of it
early on. But,
she wondered,
was it her fault or
had some wicked chance
dealt her this fate?

In college a boy
asked her out.
She was elated but
he took her to a
darkened house.

Other boys were waiting.
They laughed and
put a bag over her head.
Only wanted her
pink insides.
She managed to run.

Her heart was broken.
Another dagger
to pierce her spirit.
But deep within
she knows
she is the swan
the world

doesn't see.

She knows the
Love she has
to give.
And hope
nourishes her
that somewhere, someone
is waiting for her.

Tony Daly
VIRGINIA, USA

Tony is a poet and short-story writer of fantasy, science fiction, horror, and military fiction/non-fiction. His work has been recently published or is forthcoming with *Danse Macabre, Silverblade, The HorrorZine, Utopia Science Fiction*, and others. A retired U.S. Air Force medic, he proudly serves as an Associate Editor with *Military Experience and the Arts*.

E: aldaly13@gmail.com
W: www.aldaly13.wixsite.com/website
Twitter: @aldaly18

MEMORIES AND ANXIETIES

Vibrant colours, hanging, drooping,
like rainbows melting from a line.
Sheets of fluid happiness
blowing in the wind.
Like memories.

Memories of days in woods
singing with Thrushes and Warblers
while mother hangs laundry
from clothespins,
sings with Barry Manilow
crooning from the clock radio
strung through the open window.

Sheets hanging in the window of time,
makeshift shades hiding barren landscapes,
bleak futures behind a wall of happy.
Trapped inside painted smile,
inside fort made of vibrant sheets
patterned with rainbows,
soothing youthful anxieties
of cabin fever,

while mother kneels a thousand miles away,
inside her own retirement fort,
wailing on a cold porcelain floor,
surrounded by filth, sadness,
broken body of father sprawled, trembling,
blood oozing from fresh wound
inflicted by gravity and age.

DREAM WARRIOR

I was a weak boy-fragile in mind and body
Hiding in the corner of science class
Not speaking the language of any click
Avoiding the bullies in the halls and gym class

Then, I stood triumphant over a field
Littered with the scattered code of my enemies
Skeletons, elves, ogres, wizards, dragons,
all fell before the blade of my warrior woman

A maternal bellow from the ether returned me

to a world where I didn't belong,
A world where hunger pains wracked my fully clothed midriff,
How I prayed for a rice ball icon to appear and recover me

Yet microwaved leftovers was closest I could come.
I trudged through life, brushing my teeth, eating,

dressing in sweats instead of my armoured breastplate,
But at night I dreamed I was that warrior woman,

and hoped one day I wouldn't have to dream.

THE CELLIST

He sits upon a metallic chair, uncomfortably squirming
in pants that scratch, a dress shirt one size too small,
dress shoes one size to large, hair styled in shards,
worried about leaving his music sheet at home,
desperately waving for his teacher's attention,
but she never looks as she passes him by repeatedly
to inspect the rosined bows of violinists,
to shoo away overly attentive parents,
to check the costumes of actresses and actors.

He sits upon a metallic chair, waiting for his cue to play,
hands sweating, knees bouncing, nose itching, heart pounding,
all from nervous anxiety that floods his every thought and action,
dragging his mind into the depths of doubt and fear
from which he has inadequate practice extracting himself,
but when the wand's waved, the cords struck, the flutes blown,
his spine and fingers remember the practised positions,
the bow draws across the strings in perfect time and rhythm
producing the melodic sound that won him second seat
and the audience's adoring chatter.

David A Banks
ENGLAND

David escaped from the confines of academic writing and now roams the fresh pastures of poetry and theatre, where he encounters far less bull. He regularly earwigs on conversations in a number of café haunts under the guise of 'research'. When not reading or writing, he has been known to make wooden dolls' houses, manufacture interesting pieces of firewood on a lathe, or spend many hours in the garden planning what he might do next time the weather conditions are absolutely perfect. He lives by the wise words of a respected friend who advised that most work activities should be given 'a good coat of looking-at' before commencing.
E: traveldab@gmail.com

LONG WEEKEND

At a table by the window
in a quiet seaside cafe
two people sit together,
      but apart.

His chair sideways to her
he stares, unseeingly, outside.
      She watches him intently,
      twisting her hair into knots
      then letting it fall free.

      Almost imperceptibly,
      she shakes her head
      and tears moisten her eyes.

      Quietly she speaks to him
but her words fall on closed ears.
      Again she tries.
Again he ignores her.

Without looking at her
he pushes back his chair
and leaves the cafe.

      She hesitates,
      then follows on behind.

Two people together,
      but apart.

Linda Imbler
KANSAS, USA

Linda's published paperback poetry collections include *Big Questions, Little Sleep, Big Questions, Little Sleep: Second Edition, Lost and Found, Red Is The Sunrise,* and *Bus Lights, Travel Sights: Nashville and Back.* She has three e-books published by Soma Publishing; *The Sea's Secret Song, Pairings* - which is a hybrid e-book of short fiction and poetry - and *That Fifth Element.* Her fourth e-book entitled *Per Quindecim* will be published by Soma Publishing in 2021. Linda has been nominated for a Pushcart Prize, and has four Best Of The Net nominations. When not writing, Linda is an avid reader, classical guitar player, and a practitioner of both Yoga and Tai Chi, and helps her husband, a Luthier, build acoustic guitars.
E: mike-imbler@cox.net
W: www.lindaspoetryblog.blogspot.com

THE GLASS WINDOWS BEHIND THE PLANT

They stood together in the hall,
Each with a seemingly insurmountable fear.
He with a path so long, and the burden he carried so heavy,
She unable to lean forward from the eighth floor.

Together they promised each other,
One step at a time, one tile at a time,
Each step closer to the end of the hall,
Each tile closer to the window.

They began.
He went further,
She went further.

He channelled gazelles, swift and light,
She channelled eagles, high flying and fearless on the air.

His hospital gown trembled,
Her legs trembled.

At the end he'd walk the length several times
and had looked up and seen her smile,
At the end she had pressed her forehead
against the glass and looked down.

And he smiled back.

Eduard Schmidt-Zorner
REPUBLIC OF IRELAND / GERMANY

Eduard is a translator and writer of poetry, haibun, haiku and short stories, also under his pen-name Eadbhard McGowan. He writes in four languages: English, French, Spanish and German, and is published in over 140 anthologies, literary journals and broadsheets in the USA, the UK, Ireland, Japan, Sweden, Spain, Italy, Bangladesh, India, France, Mauritius, Nepal, Pakistan, Nigeria and Canada. Eduard holds workshops on Japanese and Chinese style poetry and prose, and experimental poetry, and some of his poems and haibun have been published in French (own translation), Romanian and Russian. Member of four writer groups in Ireland, and lives in County Kerry for more than 25 years, Eduard is a proud Irish citizen, born in Germany.

E: EadbhardMcGowan@gmx.com

REQUIEM MASS FOR CREATIVITY

More and more
we stand at graves,
live in the past and memorize,
as if the time coagulates,
becomes viscous, motionless,
does not flow, is paralysed.

Hard times for writers,
a loss:
we run out of thoughts,
impulses, ideas, emotions.
We fertilize our stories
with the past
with faint memories,
because we experience little,
nothing is happening,
the outlook so brittle
no substance for exciting poetry,
no impulse, no inspiration.

We walk with the dog
at a distance,
we avoid other humans,
see the neighbour as a threat,
we lost the trust in politicians,
religions and our fellow men.

We do not touch to feel the vibes,
no hug, no tenderness, affection,
do not receive the waves of words,
we cannot share,
we have no conversations,
no exchange of views,
a culture bogged down -
literally
from lockdown to lockdown.

What we had learnt
is lost in useless stagnation,
in self-satisfaction and
in utter isolation.

DURING THE BLITZ

Waiting in the dark, we dream of light;
deep, underground, we hear detonations,
vibrations of bombing causing fright,
impact of loads dropped on a town.

What awaits us outside is unknown,
when we inch to daylight (which we desire):
a day darkened by smoke,
or a night glowing with fire?

Grasped by fear and helplessness,
by air raids and trembling walls,
recognising nightmare's relentlessness
in the horror of today's sundown
when night falls like a gown
and sirens sound the all-clear,
in these days of war and fear,
in shelters with neighbours and strangers.

Wherever we look into dark future's night,
far from the here and now, flickering light,
far from home, hoping, and hearing
the word without knowing its meaning.

Did we see warnings looming up?
Signs on the wall, in Belshazzar's hall?
Did we anticipate tyrants, invasion, depravity?
Victims, the dead, the bombs on Coventry?

Sons of the land clothe themselves with death,
arm themselves to kill their own kind
in the places of horror, up and down the land.
Dream weavers weave a wreath,
money counters count and pay in kind;
armourers forge, steel unsheathed;
soldiers kill; leave thousands bereaved:
we are all led like puppets on a string.

In the city of lost angels,
a masked man sharpens his black scythe,
saddles his mighty horse
for the very last fight.

Burn, Phoenix, that your ashes bear fruit,
keep your heart's blood, Pelican, to feed us.
Grim Reaper has his harvest time.
We hear graveyard bells chime.

Almost filled is the hour-counting shadow glass;
nearly faded, are pottery shards with your name,
the Tree of Life, standing pale in the rain;
wilted, the rosebush that lived your love,
windblown breath that carries your words,
naked, featherless - lonely peace dove.
Go where you have never been before,
where yet so many wait.

Dianalee Velie
NEW HAMPSHIRE, USA

Dianalee is the Poet Laureate of Newbury. She is a graduate of Sarah Lawrence College, and has a Master of Arts in Writing from Manhattanville College. She is the author of six books of poetry, *Glass House, First Edition, The Many Roads to Paradise, The Alchemy of Desire, Ever After, Italian Lesson* and a collection of short stories, *Soul Proprietorship: Women in Search of Their Souls*. She is a member of the National League of American Pen Women, the New England Poetry Club, the International Woman Writers Guild, the New Hampshire Poetry Society and founder of the John Hay Poetry Society.
E: dianaleevelie@aol.com

TRUTHS

I alone cannot change the world, but I can cast a stone across the waters to create many ripples - Mother Teresa.

Truth:
I want to reverse the birth process,
grab you fresh from your mother's womb
and place you in mine. I want to rebirth
you into calm comfort, not chaos and crisis,
wrap you in a soft onesie, not harsh expectations.

Truth:
I want to buy your first prom dress,
not find you years later a sullen,
self-mutilating teenager, existing, barely,
in a group home of thugs. Thugs-
too harsh a word for those lost souls.

Truth:
Stealing you away to my home,
you slammed the door on my prayers,
turning the rap music up so loud walls shook,
daring me to discard you, throw you out
like the trash you believed you were.

Truth:
Now, body piercings, chains and foul temper
long forgotten, I am by your side,
more mother than aunt,
more proud than parent, having
birthed you from my spiritual womb
after creating for you   home.

CURRICULUM VITAE

Luxuriating in the President's oak panelled
dining room, consuming marinara sauce
over limp linguine, listening to conversation,
more flaccid than the noodles,
she flicked the grated cheese
out of her long brown hair,
her eyes lusting longingly for the door
as she gave up her ambition for tenure.

Highly flammable, combustible thoughts
exploded in her brain, probably caused
by the pre-dinner Martini.
Her faculties failing at this faculty meeting,
no longer trapped by the temptation of tenure,
she wanted to belly dance on the table,
spill her words out with each gyration
creating an unforgettable curriculum vitae
everyone would forever remember.

TRAGEDY

Green,
Lamont
murdered
grandsons
killed
daughter-in-law.
Meth
Monday
Miami
Homicide.

Black
mourning,
sobbing
family,
grieving
friends
shocked
forever.
Everywhere
grief ...

Aleksandra Vujisić
MONTENEGRO

Aleksandra is a professor of English language and literature, and a passionate writer of prose and poetry. She has participated in poetry festivals across Europe, and her works have won prizes and acknowledgements both in Montenegro and worldwide. Aleksandra writes in her native language and English, and her stories and poetry have been published several times and translated into Italian and Spanish. In 2017 she started a literary project in order to promote the importance of reading for children, and starting from May 2021 she is a member of the Association of Montenegrin authors for children.

E: Aleksandra.vujisic@gmail.com

FUTURE

I woke up this morning
asking the yesterday's fears to leave.
I was thinking about all the
lovers that need some time to forgive -
and now, don't ask me what I will
think tomorrow,
it is hard to know the future,
names of joy and the sorrow.

I woke up this morning
full of old music and new hope,
like a dog holding to its torturers
and not letting of the rope -
and now, don't ask me if I
will bark to the stars,
it is hard to know the future,
and how it heals the old scars.

I woke up this morning
asking the yesterday's promises to leave.
I was thinking of new days
and the old ones that still grieve -
and now, don't ask me where I will
be breathing,
for all the future pains - my heart won't
be longer bleeding.

Maria Nemy Lou Rocio
HONG KONG / PHILIPPINES

Maria is from the Philippines and currently working in Hong Kong. She started to write poetry when she was in High School, but only found her way back into writing three years ago, when she started to work abroad. She expresses her thoughts and emotions through writing poetry and short stories, and as a way of overcoming the trials of being separated from her family. She is an active member of 'Arts in Me', a writing platform in Singapore founded by The Migrant Writers of Singapore, and is a team-leader of Uplifters, a non-profit, non-government organization in Hong Kong that gives free online money management courses.

E: misnemz@gmail.com
FB: @Marias-Corner-My-Poem-My-Story-103973511564918

ME

I had braved many storms
And every time, I adjusted my sail
Passing through without sinking
I am the captain of my ship

I spread my wings and soar
Facing rough winds above
There were turbulences but never crashed
I am the pilot of my own flight

I've been to war zone
A soldier of full valour
Fighting with a brave heart
I am the commander of my own battle

Into the forest I ventured
I will never become a prey
One of the fittest among the herd
I am the Tigress, the hunter in my own jungle

Time has made me what I am today
Failures had given me wisdom
My yesterday's subdues are my tomorrow's triumphs
I am me, this is me, I am the queen of my life

Rezauddin Stalin
BANGLADESH

Former Deputy Director of Nazrul Institute, and senior editor of *Magic Lonthon* - a literary organization – award-winning writer and poet Rezauddin Stalin is a well-known TV anchor and media personality, and the founder and chairman of the Performing Art Centre. He has published more than 100 books, many of which have been translated worldwide. His awards include; Darjeeling Natto Chokhro Award, India (1985), Bangla Academy (2006), Micheal Modhushudhan Dutta Award (2009), Shobho Shachi Award, West Bengal (2011), Torongo of California Award, USA (2012), Writers Club Award, California, USA (2012), Badam Cultural Award, California, USA (2012), City Ananda Alo Award (2015), West Bengal Centre Stage Barashat Award (2018), Journalist Association Award, UK (2018) and Silk Road Poet Laureate Award Xi'an China (2020).
E: rezauddinstalin@gmail.com
W: www.nazrulinstitute.gov.bd
Wikipedia: @Rezauddin_Stalin

THE COMMAND

Mother commanded, open the window, child,
the mist of downpour has filled the room with darkness.

Mother, the downpour has not yet ceased, I said
Lightning is flashing continually outside.
Any moment our shelter may collapse.

Frightened at my words, everyone in the house said,
Let us move out,
The old walls are not reliable.
I said the curfew is in force outside
how can you move out of doors?
The hungry peasants of the village
are invading the town again and again.
They are legions
and the sentinels of the town will possible be overpowered.

Everyone's mouth was dry with anxiety.
What good will it do them to invade the town?
I said, they want to take possession of the town,
the accumulation of their labours.
If they think it necessary, they will have no qualms
about killing us.

Mother said, the peasants in the village
are simple folk.
They can never be so ruthless.
Besides, I am from their village
they will surely pay regard to this.

My younger sister's conviction is that
since on day she gave water to a thirsty peasant
he will save her.

My younger brother said
I once doled out a few coins to a hungry peasant
to buy bread.
if he is in the group
he will not assassinate me a least.

Now everyone looked towards me.
But I could lay claim to no redemptive deed

that would save me.
Knowing this, everyone in sorrow and remorse
commanded me again to open the window.

John Tunaley
ENGLAND

John was born in Manchester in 1945. Father: foundry hand, mother; crane-driver is what his birth certificate states ... (the war was a melting pot ... throwing them together at the steel works). He now lives in Robin Hood's Bay, North Yorkshire. He's in a few writing groups ... (Natalie keeps the Whitby Library Writing Group blog up to date ... it's too tricky for John). He sticks to sonnets, as the form exercises some control of his worst excesses. They pile up ... the excesses ... He likes anthologies ... he enjoys the company ... (and there's safety in numbers ...).
E: johntunaley@yahoo.co.uk

THE SECOND ARROW
The 'Appointment Letter' Dream

She entrusts a sheaf of letters to me ...
... the names and addresses written in an
ancient but legible script ... in black ink
with a scratchy pen. She sees I'm distressed ...
... (a gentle motion with her hand ... the palm
open ... the fingers relaxed). I will not
get lost ... the path is along the side of
the canal. However long or curved ...
... I'm bound to pass the various dwellings.
Late afternoon or early evening?
I'm uncertain ... the mild grey sky reveals
little ... some slight tonal variations,
with light and dark snakings. I try not to worry ...
... that dismissing gesture was meant to reassure ...

THE THIRD ARROW
Waiting for the Appointment

Today, York is as quiet as my village.
You can hear the birds sing on the clear air ...
... (not larks)... sparrows mostly but there's a fair
number of jackdaws give a raw, rough edge
to the age-old chorus. The sky is fleeced
with blue between the white ... a blackbird strikes
up ... and one more far-off. Wall walkers hike
past ... hidden behind the new seasons pieced
patchwork of leaves. A police car siren, jet
plane and Minster bell introduce themselves,
(a contrapuntal episode that serves
to emphasise the hush). A robin sets
itself in an enquiring position ...
... attracting crumbs without volition ...

THE FOURTH ARROW
The 'Ploughing Match ' Dream

The field is revealed ... there's no grass ... just soil ...
... which lies in irregular crescent shaped
drifts. Where to start? Stood at one side, I am
bewildered ... the horses are willing and
strong ... the ploughshare sharp and shining but it
is clear that the ground first needs levelling.
It's not a life-or-death task ... is it? More
an exhibition ... a working display ...
I don't need it billiard-table flat,
just something that won't topple us over.
If I could identify the borders ...
... find out where I might start, (and stop), the job.
Furrows parallel to at least one side? Rather
than aimless endless spirals, might also make sense.

Anne Maureen Medrano Esperidion
HONG KONG / PHILIPPINES

Anne is Filipino but currently working as a domestic helper in Hong Kong. Her passion for poetry started in her elementary school days, and uses her poems as her personal medium of communicating and expressing her thoughts, ideas and emotions.
E: maureenanne090188@gmail.com
FB: @annemaureen.medranoesperidion

ADVERSITIES

Agony, trials and afflictions
Dreadful events that stripped us
Ventures of defeat and failures
Entangled us to struggles and strife
Roller-coaster of unfortunate events
Suppressing our perseverance and stillness
Imprisoned us into the darkness
Trapped us into the pit of torment
Indeed so anguished yet we are not fighting alone
Every battle we have God always with us
Sending us with His profound love

Rahim Karim
KYRGYZSTAN

Author of the national bestseller *Kamila*, Rahim is an Uzbek-Kyrgyz-Russian Soviet poet, writer, publicist and translator. A Graduate of the Maxim Gorky Literature Institute, Moscow, Rahim is a member of a large numbers of national and international literary associates including: the National Union of Writers of the Kyrgyz Republic, the Union of Journalists of the Kyrgyz Republic. He has won a large number of literary awards including: Author of the Year - 2019 (Netherlands), Author of the Year - 2019 (Montenegro), Author of the Year – 2019 (USA), and World Literature Icon (Mexico/India). His work has been published around the world including in Uzbekistan, Kazakhstan, Hungary, Ukraine, Belarus, Russia, Azerbaijan, Great Britain, Canada, Mongolia, Romania, Greece, the Netherlands, Zimbabwe, and many others. He has translated poetry and prose into Uzbek, Russian, Kyrgyz and English by authors in almost 30 countries. He worked as editor-in-chief of the *Golos Tekstilshchika* newspaper (Osh), deputy editor-in-chief of the city newspaper *Vecherniy Osh*, own correspondent of the *Khalk Suzi* newspaper of the Supreme Council of Uzbekistan in Kyrgyzstan, editor-in-chief of the regional newspaper *Ak-Buura*, executive secretary of the international literary fiction almanac *Osh*, a leading specialist of the Osh regional department of culture, editor-translator of the AKIpress Information and Analytical Bureau, and editor-in-chief of the Central Asian news service *Canews*.
E: kamron2003@mail.ru
FB:@rahimkarimov1960
Wikipedia: @Каримов,_Рахим

IT HAS BEEN HARD ...

It was hard for me to live in this world
Among deceit, lies, rumours, treason.
I was saving myself, drowning, with a lyre,
Freed from waves and foam.
The interpretation did not give rest,
Crafty that the heart tore out.
A lie, a lie, a magpie coo,
Truth upside down
Oh how cynical the people of this world are
Weave from nothing that the fabric is ready.
Serpentine tongue during a feast,
Sting, so that everyone is ready.
I was ready to wrest from the untruth of life,
Blood boiled in me like a wave of the sea.
There was so much slime all around me
From what I tasted grief.
Unable to resist was the fallen,
Weightlessness kept me honoured.
I was tired to look at the lost,
Forgive them, God, if they did not have a conscience!

Sazma Samir
AUSTRALIA / SINGAPORE

Of Indian heritage, growing up in Singapore, Sazma is currently a 19 year old student at the University of Wollongong, Australia. At 16 she published her first book - after 4 years of work. Her writing style continues to evolve and grow, branching out from the Fantasy-Fiction genre to poetry and short prose, thanks to the influence of her love for literature cultivated in classrooms during her secondary years. Her poetry is deeply influenced by modern issues, as well as her own experiences as a young adult in chaotic times.
E: sazma2002@gmail.com

NO APOLOGIES

By my side you stood
Resolute and unwavering.
Through the wars and victories
We persevered through.

I grew used to your presence.
A constant source of stability
Through the chaos of heaven and hell.
I grew complacent and greedy
Took your grace for granted
And returned less in kind.

We speak different languages
But eyes don't lie.
And I hope when you see mine
You know I will always stand by your side

EARTH

Built on unsteady foundations
Of fiery magma and stubborn rock
The earth spins on an axis
In the expanse of nothingness
Life spawned from infertile grounds
And found how to survive.
Mechanisms creaking, words spoken
We hurt each other
without seeing the pain, it caused
People made of complexities

BROKEN BUT NOT SHATTERED

Beware of those with those dull eyes and messy hair
Beware of those who walk with shoulders slouched and alone
Shadowy figures of what once were human
Beware of those with tight smiles that seem like they don't even have faces
Faceless and nameless souls with the husk of a human

Beware of those who sit alone, in their rooms bare
Their mind, body and soul left to stare
Skin marred with scars left from when they were alone
Memories scarring their mind, body and soul

—

Rich Orloff

NEW YORK, USA

Rich's short plays have had over 2000 productions on six continents - and a staged reading in Antarctica. His poetry cycle for performance, *Blessings from the Pandemic,* has been produced by theatres, schools, churches and synagogues, was published by TRW Plays. During the year until the pandemic struck, Rich travelled around the United States performing his one-person show *It's a Beautiful Wound*, about his experience in underground, psychedelic-assisted therapy. Primarily a playwright, *The New York Times* called his play *Big Boys* "rip-roaringly funny" and named *Funny as a Crutch* a Critic's Pick.
E: richplays@gmail.com
W: www.richorloff.com
W: www.trwplays.com

A PRAYER WHILE ROWING

Like someone alone
in a rowboat
in the middle of a sea
of unknown length
I keep rowing
and dreaming of standing
on firm ground again

I cannot turn back
I cannot rush my journey
There will be storms
There will be calm

Sometimes I think I couldn't have it worse
But then I remember
I have a boat
I have oars
I may not be on firm ground
But I have a vessel and I have tools
And stronger arms than I ever knew I had

When I reach my destination
My blistered soul will need healing
But I haven't arrived yet
So I keep rowing
One stroke at a time
Dreaming of the future
Accepting of the now

First published in *Blessings from the Pandemic*.

Volkan Hacıoğlu
TURKEY

Volkan received Bachelor of Arts in 2000, and Master of Arts in 2003 and a Ph.D. In 2010, and lectures courses on Aesthetics at Nazim Hikmet Academy. His poems, essays on poetry, and poetry translations appeared in various international and national journals and magazines. He has eight books of poetry published, and won several international poetry awards. He was the-editor-in-chief of the international multilingual magazine *Rosetta World Literatura*. His books include: *Duvarlarda Gözlerim Üşüyor* (2006), *Dansa Kaldırılmayan Kadın* (2010), *Ahenk Kapısı* (2013), *Budapeşte Radyosu* (2016), *Şehri Terk Eden Hayalet* (2017), *Doğu Hindistan Kumpanyası* (2017), *Zerdüşt ve Kırlangıç* (2018), *Unutulmuş Aryalar* (2019); *şiir çevirileri: Anarşinin Maskesi,* (Percy Bysshe Shelley, 2010); *Neşideler,* (Behruz Kia, 2013); *Seçilmiş Şiirler,* (Ralph Waldo Emerson, 2016); *Şiirler,* (Ralph Hodgson, 2016); *deneme-inceleme: Köşeli Parantez* (Sanat ve Edebiyat Yazıları 2016) and *Poetik Meditasyonlar* (2018).
E: volkan_hacioglu@yahoo.com
W: www.volkanhacioglu.wixsite.com/thepoet
FB: @616784647
Instagram: @volkan_hacioglu
Twitter: @volkanthepoet

THE DAGGER OF CHATEAUBRIAND

Those said are not that much important.
And also those that are not said ...
One ought to look at the things done and undone.
More important is to read behaviour and action.

To understand moves.
Moves of sword and pen.
The real wars are not waged between people.
Characters clash most of the time.
Beyond grave and everywhere.

One becomes late, the other does not wait.
Here you are! A wordless dialogue.
One neglects, the other betrays.
Here you are! A wordless monologue.
Possibility, probability and likelihood.

The poetry is writ not with words but with mute letters.

After months arrives Chateaubriand
To the château bought for him by his lover
And on the fireplace with his dagger
He scratches two verses.

And then departs from the château.
His lover never forgets those verses till she dies.

THE REVENGE OF CAESAR

The Roman General Julius Caesar
In the year seventy five before Christ
By crossing over the broken amphoras
Was going to Greece on the galleys of history.

As he flee from the tyranny of Sulla
Who decisively defeated at the Black Sea
Mithridates the Great, the king of Pontus
And declared himself dictator.

In the turbulent waters of Mediterranean
Young Caesar is held captive by the pirates,
Only to be set free in return for ransom
And he is taken as hostage of buccaneers.

So little seemed to the eyes of Caesar
Twenty golden tokens of Roman coins
Hence he swore and promised for revenge
The General who says I at least worth fifty.

As soon as he get rid of the hands of bandits
He was without cease saying that he will return
And kill them all whilst he was under the captivity
Ransomers thought the hostage was making joke.

Caesar kept his promise when he is released
Ere long came back and killed all of the pirates
By crossing over the broken amphoras
As he returns to Rome on the galleys of history.

THE MISTAKE OF EINSTEIN

I put all the books of sorcery on the table
And lit a candle that melts the tears of Frankenstein
And then thought of you, and suddenly understood
Where Einstein made the mistake.

The matter equals the poverty of philosophy.
Here velocity of light. Here speed of my heart.
Here love. Here loneliness.
Here stars. Here dawn.
Here hypnotic look of Cleopatra.

Some accidents are destiny of some trains.
The seventh cigarette that Nâzım lighted
Whilst writing "Turns Out That I Had Loved," the poem
Of loves he had discovered aboard Prag-Berlin train.
The geometry was constant in this question.

Your hands in my hands are a Rodin statue.
The gravitational force of your eyes
Razes temples to the ground.
The matter equals a rose in pieces.
Caressed hairs on the doorsills.
The courage of thunders on the mirrors.
Through the absenteeism of lost sees
My spirit beheld an immortal picture.

Ermira Mitre Kokomani
NEW JERSEY, USA

Ermira is a bilingual poet, essayist and translator. She has published poetry, short stories and scientific papers in Albania and the US. Last year her book of poetry *The Soul's Gravity* was published in Albanian. Her poetry has appeared in *Jerry Jazz Musician,* (New York, 2020), *Sequoyah Cherokee River Journal 7,* (October, 2020), *Live Encounters,* (December, 2020), CAPS book *Mightier-Poets for Social Justice* (New York, 2020), and international anthologies *Musings during a Pandemic, I Can't Breathe* (Kistrech Poetry Festival, Kenya, 2020), *Rutherford Red Wheelbarrow 13,* (New Jersey, 2020), *A New World, Mediterranean Poetry 2019,* Montclair Write Group anthology, *NJ 2018,* Brownstone Poets anthology, and a range of other print and online publications. Ermira has also translated from Albanian into English the fiction novel *The King's Shadow,* authored by Viktor Canosinaj. She has majored in English Language, and has taught writing in NJ colleges for some years. She works for Rutgers University libraries, is a member of Montclair Writers' Group and Red Wheelbarrow Poet, and regularly reads her poetry in Open Mic events in New Jersey, New York, and France.
E: emitre1@yahoo.com

TIMES OF BLIZZARD

Suddenly,
our life's sack of routines is twisted,
broken and torn by the unexpected.
All mortals hang on a wire
no longer strong and rigid,
but strident, cold and brittle.
Little by little,
loosening the knot
that keeps us together.
The virus, as a mole
crumbling our lungs
is still walking alive
in our breaths,
strong and dangerous,
We have been weak,
extremely weak,
allowing it to expand,
drying the rivers in land
taking over our lives
in an uncharted path.
Feeling sad isn't enough.
Defeat carved on tombstones,
is not just a scar on the dirt,
resisting new routines is unfair,
beholding self a Cherubim of Paradise
in our frantic world is mere fantasy,
calibrating other ways as 3-W
is a challenge to win over the ignorance
in our times of blizzard!

OUR COMPLICATED EGO

Being together with you in this room,
is like looking at a convex mirror.
I keep telling you to drop the negative focal length
of your attitude, which persists diverging the light away.
Hence, the walls agree to me, witnessing your game.
Your piercing eye as a blazed sword
rushes to cut the neuron cord in my brain
that connects my thoughts and language,
just to trick and dump my tongue loose
in your trap of absurd gibberish.
Instead, as a Victorian woman of modern times,
in my subconscious mind, I call my resistance,
to prison my thoughts in my mind's cage,
while holding my breath in the lung's detention
and handcuffing that moving paddle of flesh in the cell
between the jaws' walls not to release a corrupted word.
On the back of shining surface of the mirror,
the dark, gloomy side of the poisonous mercury
of your thoughts raises its head and depicts my face
as misshaped, diverging and demeaning its beauty.
I can see your shadow,
a montage-like imprint of your character,
hidden behind the glass of your convex mirror.
it's just "the power of my third eye", in action
that you can hardly grasp.

Unfortunately,
your pattern walks in front of me every day.
I look at it and shake my head,
silence wraps my essence in a monologue:
How can Ego shine so brightly in an inverse mode,
and eat you like an apple, bite after bite,
until there is no more flesh left,
but the hard core protecting the seeds,
in the submerge.
Your selfish teeth lack the courage
to break the hard substance.
They carry fear!
But, I don't!
It's called Resistance to Corruption!

I offer you my tower of power

build on stones of quietness and peace.
Instead of reacting to your muddy thoughts,
I dwell inside myself, quietly,
and offer you the silent companion,
who starts eating the edges of stillness,
bit by bit, crunch by crunch,
as if I am eating the apple of silence,
in the brink of its existence;
until I reach the depth and
touch the hard core of myself,
sheltering the seeds of hope and rebirth.
I meet and hear the solar plexus speaking to me
and responding to your scornful thoughts:
"That core remains untouched to recreate."
Can you hear it? If you don't,
reverse your hearing and listen:
My silence is the strength that fails you,
you cannot scramble or tear it down
or undo my fine soul.
Thus, your Ego can never Undo Me.
My untouched core rejects you loudly:
Even if you dare to rip my skin,
and grind my bones into powder,
or drink my blood, as the rarest tasteful wine,
in a cup made of Japanese porcelain,
that you used to water roses
the only humans you cared for;
even if you dared to turn me into ashes,
my pure soul will rise again like a phoenix
and fly to burn your piercing look,
and melt the venom metal off your mirror.
Then, there will be quietness in the room,
the walls will cheer up and smile in your absence.

First published *Sequoyah Cherokee River Journal*, 2020.

Mark O. Decker
DELAWARE, USA

Mark is a retired businessman, who started writing poetry beginning in 1968, and continues to the present. After retiring, in 2016, he decided to organize his life's work of poetry in order to preserve it for his children and grandchildren. As a result, he started self-publishing his poetry in 2016, and to-date has self-published fifteen books of poetry. He concurrently started sharing some of his poetry with his family and friends. Because of the very positive reaction he received about his poetry from family and friends, and through a writer's group he belongs to in Virginia and Delaware, he decided that he would share his words with a broader audience.

E: mdeckersr@gmail.com
FB: @Mark O. Decker Sr
Instagam: @Okeypoet

LISTEN TO THE WORDS

Words flow like streams
and rivers;
They have meaning,
they have sound;
Some are square,
some are round;
They have speed;
I listen for them,
to them;
They guide me
when the path is dark;
They hide me
from the demons,
help me find the reasons
to put one foot
in front of the other,
they tell me
I'm their brother;
So, listen with me,
you will hear the sound,
you will grow to know
life's happiness and frowns.

Sandy Phillips
ENGLAND

Sandy has always loved the arts, especially the written word, painting and sculpture. Along with her church, these have kept her busy in her retirement. She belongs to two poetry groups, and two art groups; *The Monday Painters* and the *Enfield Art Circle,* and she once had a clay sculpture in the Royal Academy. She has written articles for psychic magazines, and her book about her life in spirit is titled: *The Narrow Doorway*.
E: sandy.phillips72@yahoo.co.uk

MISFORTUNE

The eyes narrow into slits, through which an unreal world
.appears all disjointed; nothing quite makes sense. Like a
doomed forecast, the sky is falling, pulling black clouds down.
 Brows knit into furrows, and a headache begins.

Tense wires strain and are held taut from the depths, they
reverberate through the skull making it heavy.
It appears as if the whole world is set against you.
Could I confide in a friend or family? I wonder.

They really wouldn't help anyway, it's my problem.
They'd spout all the age old platitudes: and would I really want
 the entire population to know my business? No!
There must be a solution. I curl into a natal coil.

Adversity should make the energy flow into combat status instead
 of cowering beneath a blanket. Come on girl, pull yourself together,
face it. Who was it that said, a coward dies a thousand times before
 his death, the valiant taste death but once.

So, with this in mind I rise and face my misfortune and
dress in my bright red clothes for courage and energy,
apply my facial war paint and look for spiritual help to aid
my purpose; thus armed I stride out into the day ahead.

Lorraine Sicelo Mangena
ZIMBABWE

Twenty year-old Lorraine resides In Bulawayo. She is currently a first year student at the National University of Science and Technology (NUST) in Bulawayo, pursuing her bachelor's degree in Journalism and Media Studies. She is a passionate poet who has great dreams in the world of literature. Her journey of poetry has just started, and she has, so far, managed to pen down 18 poems yet to be published.
E: mathemaprince20@gmail.com
FB: @lorraine.sicelo

GRACEFULLY BROKEN

Beyond an emotional betrayal, tears never divorced my life.
Like winter, so frozen was my heart;
I laid my head on a rock and gave a pillow to the feet.
Poverty, Poverty, Poverty.
Sophisticated to jail the wishes of a beggar,
Why dim the sun to mislead my dreams?
I was lusting after the champagne but you poured me vinegar,
You suffocated my joy in a concealed envelope of deception,
And sang lullabies of poisoned lyrics.
You are the wind that blew away my umbrella to let the rains wash away my visions,
You stripped my regalia and told them I was insane.
Like a mummified corpse I was reluctant to rescue myself,
When humans threw me to the wilderness;
Toes unable to grip, I strived to ride a giraffe and scrutinised the future,
Revelations, Revelations, Revelations.
Some hope glittered on waves of divine waters,
I saw the green grass stretching taller than yesterday,
Ready to renovate my nest;
I accommodated the journey of misery,
And earned the enthusiasm of my feathers;
Prosperity, Prosperity, Prosperity.

Gabriela Docan
ENGLAND / ROMANIA

Gabriela is a humanist, poet, nature lover, chronic daydreamer, over thinker, traveller, with joy of life and admiration for all things that are beautiful. Many things inspire her to write, such as a memory, a song, a nature walk, a personal experience, people, romantic relationships, inner struggles and her work experience in mental health. Her poems have been published by Writer's Egg Magazine, Spillwords.com and various print anthologies.
E: gabriela_docan@yahoo.com

A WINTER TALE

A heavy winter stormed the flesh,
blood flow froze ferociously
like waterfalls in Iceland.

I was burning like hot lava
bubbling beneath the ground,
but felt only frozen.

Streams of sweat surfaced skin,
strong shivers shook my spine,
I then succumbed into long sleep.

So many nights of discontent,
sunken in near-death sleep
in the darkest of all winters.

I drowned in daunting darkness,
dwelled on fears of death,
like a doomed sleeping beauty.

Mean migraines mauled the mind
in monstrous, meaningless attacks
like dogs with a bone.

Then a callous cough creeped in,
that crippled the chirping of voice
into shreds of squeaky sounds.

A fecund fatigue slowly ferments
inside the trenches of ill flesh,
while dollops of time drop dead.

ON THE RUN

Worry hunts him like a lioness,
waiting for a moment of weakness
when she can strike
and feast on his brain.

She lets him regain strength for a while,
before attacking ferociously.
Every day he is on the run:
taken down imminently and eaten alive.

Her teeth dig into his flesh,
rip out his inner peace
and crush it under her strong jaws,
leaving him totally drained.

Most plans of the day get slashed
by gruelling dark anticipations,
making him sweat and breathe fast,
until he chokes with anxiety.

Sometimes he stops running,
to seek a brief moment of peace,
when he can heal his wounds,
while keeping a close eye on the lioness.

He looks for threats from his watchtower
with unnecessary vigilance,
patrolling like a sergeant
in defence of the inner peace.

Deploying incommensurable forces
against an army of worries
is his never-ending bloodless fight,
most times invisible to the eye.

THE MIND'S KNOTS

I anticipate everything before it begins,
Imagine worst scenarios when the mind spins,
I become sick with worry, doubt, countless fears,
The inner peace then eventually disappears.

Being in the spotlight is something I dread,
I struggle to concentrate on what's being said.
I get nervous, shaky, stumble upon words,
As my attention is focused deeply inwards.

I want to do many things, but I am held back,
Immobilized by tentacles of the anxiety attack;
I am feeling light-headed and about to faint;
I freeze when all I want is to live without restraint.

Hope gets often shattered during this fight,
But I know calm follows after each high tide.
I breathe in and out, silence unhelpful thoughts,
Try to untie the mind's overwhelming knots.

William Conelly
ENGLAND / USA

After completing military service in the US Air Force, William took a master's degree in English literature from the University of California. Work took William and his family to England in 2003, and seven years later they became British citizens. Able Muse publishes a collection of his lyric verse titled *Uncontested Grounds*, and in April, 2021, Olympia Press brought out an illustrated book of his poems for children titled *West Of Boston*.
E: wmconelly@yahoo.com

HEAVY SNOW PREDICTED

*For three voices, deep in
forested Massachusetts*

'Take off the satin jacket, George; forget
the vampire Christmas tie — scarlet and black
on virgin white — today's work clothes are fine.'

'The business-looks okay for you, Bernice.
You worked at home. My suit and I spent Friday
digging through a High Street paper mine.'

'Mom stop pretending you're in charge.
Dad doesn't need his uniform at night.
He's lots more human with a purple shine.'

'Todd, looking closer, I see your Mom's right.
With boss, associates, and drinks on hand,
my evening wear should tow the firm's midline.'

'Your father's not in high school, Todd. Panache
won't benefit our family's long-term goals,
no matter how your favourite styles incline.'

'Right, Mom. Tell me I'm queer. Tell me stay home
and shovel snow. You, Dad and John shove off.
I'll clean the walk and drive, then take strychnine.'

'Look closer, Todd: the satin sheen you fancy's
faded on my shoulders: standard outcome
for a fabric closeted past prime.'

'You take Dad's jacket, Todd. It's a near fit.
Check the watch pocket. Find a fiver, did you?
Splurge on licorice Monday, after school time.'

'You're both brain sops. I can't believe I share
genetic code with you. I'll take the five
for shovelling and building up my spine.'

'Your night's off, John! You're brother-sitting Todd!
He's clearing snow outside! Fetch him indoors
if he weakens, faints or ices over supine!'

'George, warm the engine. Todd, broom the windscreen.
We'll nudge right through these drifts. What's with the looks?
Am I this winter's Bride of Frankenstein?'

'One lane's half clear. You'll meet the plough head on.
You'll ride reverse — sliding, swerving — right back here.
The blizzard curtain's closed. It's family time.'

Sharon Harper
MISSOURI, USA

Sharon lives in Missouri with poodles and cicadas, and long hot summer days. She writes for a sense of clarity and fascination and wonder. Besides words Sharon also likes to sculpt clay and figure out ideas in mixed media drawing.

E: SharonHarper@MissouriState.edu

SCAVENGER

My grief is a nagging crow
revisiting the empty feeder and screaming for more.
It rips the last greasy bite of suet from
the empty cage while swinging
by a toenail in the wind.
Remnants of black oil sunflower seeds litter the ground like
hundreds of dead beetles matting down the grass.
The squirrels rummage through the discards
like me when I visit the Goodwill and linger over all the
unwanted objects of other people's dead relatives .
My grief walks the aisles with me
as I find a flowered comforter like my mother's and
I am reminded of my brother's fascination with mail order knives.

My grief pecks at me when I turn out the light
and wrap myself in the purple quilt I made
after my relationship died.
I close my eyes in defence
but there is none.
My sadness is written in charcoal
and rubs itself into my sheets-it chafes my skin
and irritates my lungs.

The crow shrieks and lifts into the darkness.
Tomorrow I will throw torn stale bread into the yard
as an offering.

FILTERING LIGHT

Inside I am full of screen
like the breezeway door.
I am filtering the incandescent light coming
from the 1960's fixture with twin shades on the wall.

The fish fry smells fill
the room and roll through the screen of the
jalousie window spilling into the lakeside yard in front of the cabin.
The men went fishing today and
Henry fileted each one with surgical precision.

Not like when John and I went fishing and
laughed so hard as we butchered each fish we caught
leaving a bucket of carnage and no
perceptible food behind.
Just mangled guts and random fins and skin
laying on the ground around us.
We ultimately had to give up and go to the Circle Inn for dinner that
night.

Henry's work was a grand pile of tiny perch filets mother
flour coated and
Fried crisp in cast iron skillets.
She hoped to bring proper reverence to one of his
only gifts.
She set a piece of bread by each plate in case a
wayward bone lodged
in our throats.

My screen collected all the
Barbed hooks dished up that night as she laughed about
my teenage hope chest being a hopeless chest
with my lake perch dinner
On melamine plates.
 She passed Henry the corn on the cob
hoping he would look up from the corn to see her
and stay.

I knock over my diet rite bottle soaking
my dinner and mother says, "good one Grace,get a dish rag".

We have strawberry shortcake for dessert.

Henry polishes off two bowls
before he leaves again.

Andrei Pershin
RUSSIA

Andrei is the author of articles on physics, philosophy and literature, several books of poetry and various photo projects (in Russia, UK and Poland). His poetry in English has appeared in a number of publications.
E: pershin.andrew@gmail.com

ADVERSITY

*

pain is an empty pearl
in thousands of layers
takes away from the best a thousand times
takes you to the depths
where there is no shine
there is no even a dark grain
or random dust
but only emptiness
transforming everything
into pearl

*

there are kinds of light
that you never get tired of observing
and others
that you tired hoping for

you understand that all of this is light
because both of them
essentially the same

*

enough
I tell myself from day to day
in the midst of something regular
the sleep or food or speech
not surprising
that it's so hard to say enough
to what was not at all

*

the past can accelerate
(when different fruits
end up on the same branch)
or it can become music – when
silence flows

worse if
the past starts to speak
but this fear – passes

*

through the smoke I see the light also
far from the fire
how many of those who are not here
how long until the morning

the moon was wandering the corners
was turning the lanterns off
but without the moon I know by myself
that this is the very edge of the earth

*

and I suddenly remembered that I was flying
in a dream without fear and storyline
and miraculous rift
overcame by this memory

now I would forget that I loved ...
this is too rational zeal
jump forward with all the strength
to get beyond the verge of a poem

Amelia Fielden
AUSTRALIA

Amelia writes mainly in the Japanese traditional forms of tanka and tanka prose. She lives in Wollongong, a coastal city in eastern Australia, where she enjoys beach-wandering and the ever-changing ocean scenery.
E: anafielden@gmail.com

TILL WE MEET AGAIN

a lone surfer
riding grey-green waves
this long morning
I wait on the beach
for the clouds to roll by

Pandemic weather hangs over fortress Australia as normal life stalls.
Once more there are separations from loved ones.

Part of every war, such separations.

four ships anchored
along the horizon
storm clouds mass
more restrictions
Delta still winning

During World War I, believed to be 'the war to end all wars', an
American popular song* was:

"When the clouds roll by, I'll come to you
Then the skies will seem more blue
... Till we meet again"

day's end sky
fading blue,streaked pink and gold
wraps this city
quietened by Covid lockdown ...
what colour might hope be?

*Till We Meet Again,1918 ; lyrics by Raymond B.Egan,music by Richard A.Whiting.

Bhuwan Thapaliya
NEPAL

Bhuwan is the author of four poetry collections *Safa Tempo: Poems New and Selected, Our Nepal, Our Pride, Rhythm of the Heart* and *Verses from the Himalayas*, and is currently working on his latest collection *The Marching Millions*. He has read his poetry and attended seminars in venues around the world including: South Korea, the USA, Thailand, Cambodia, and Nepal, and his work has been widely published in leading literary journals, newspapers and periodicals such as *Kritya, The Foundling Review, ApekshaNews, Strong Verse, Counercurrents.org, myrepublica, The Kashmir Pulse, Taj Mahal Review, Nuveine Magazine, Poetry Life and Times, Ponder Savant, VOICES(Education Project), The Vallance Review, Longfellow Literary Project, Poets Against the War* and others. His poetries have also been published in CDs and books including: *The New Pleiades Anthology of Poetry , Tonight: An Anthology of World Love Poetry and The Strand Book of International Poets 2010* and many more.
E: nepalipoet@yahoo.com

TRUDGING UP

Forlorn in the lethal frozen slopes
just a few meters beneath
the summit of my dreams
I bowed down with exhaustion,
in a cold, gritty wind.
Exhausted, with hope-tipped
mountaineering sticks in hands,
I wondered about my ancestor's life
behind the blue door of the sky cabinets
and saw clothes of my ancestors fluttering
on a half broken clotheslines in the sky.
My vision slowly distorted,
an attitude sickness
or maybe more.
I coughed thrice, and suddenly
the spirit of my long lost dreams
in the canyons of the realism
rose from their siesta and danced
around me shouting brisk words
of encouragement.
"Don't give up, it's only
a mere altitude headache
you will get over it,"
they kept on chanting.
I stood shakily
and found myself
trudging up
my dreams
gravelly trails
once again.

Barbara Webb
ENGLAND

Barbara lives in Kent, which is where she retired to some while ago. She is very new to poetry, having only started writing within the past few months.
E: barbarawebb278@gmail.com

NEVER GIVE UP

Never give up when times are hard
Don't get too down when life is tough
Put your best foot forward and deal with
Whatever comes along when it's rough

When confronted with a very high wall
Just when everything seemed so sound
You might feel you can't climb any higher
Don't despair, there is always a way round

Sometimes you feel as if you can't go on
When the pain is too difficult to bear
The helplessness that overcomes you
Is always something that can be shared

Don't hide away when life is a struggle
Let friends know just how you are feeling
Those that care will always be there
To offer the help that you are needing

No matter what washes up your way
Simply swim with the tide, do not drown
Soon you will be riding the crest of a wave
Coming through that feeling of sinking down

You will need grit and dogged determination
Use all your courage and prepare for a fight
The pride you will feel when you conquer
Will bring that welcome vision of hope to light

At the start of a race it is hard to know
Exactly how you are going to do
Just keep that winner's tape in sight
It is waiting there for you to burst through

It's so easy to wallow in self-pity and
Bury yourself in a chasm of decline
That winning smile will appear again
Once you come through and cross that line

Jenny Brown
ENGLAND

Jenny was born in apartheid South Africa, where her parents were active in the ANC. Her family moved to London after her father was a political prisoner in The Old Fort, the Johannesburg prison for White men. South Africa and politics have remained important to Jenny throughout her life. She began writing poetry and songs in her twenties, was an active education campaigner for decades, and was twice interviewed on *Newsnight*. Jenny took Open University courses, while working as a teaching assistant and becoming a teacher herself aged 50. Since retirement in 2014, Jenny has contributed to local activism, dug out her shelved anthologies, and joined a local poetry writing group. Her poems are influenced by nature, relationships and injustice. Jenny enjoys writing poems that reveal, as well as those that heal.
E: jenny29brown@hotmail.co.uk

MY BAG OF ADVERSITY

I carry my bag of adversity awkwardly.
It will not let me put it down, so it stays knowingly.
Occasionally, letting in times of calm,
Despite delayed shock bringing harm.
I talk on paper through writing in ink,
Using small steps, anchored to a secure link.

Seeking harmony, I find conflict,
Discord finds me to be an easy target.
Anger rages at the accident.
Injustice reverberating.
My nervous system crackling,
Like fire, in a furnace of stress.

With time, I bring compassion to myself,
No comparisons with anyone else,
The weight of a bag of adversity differs,
The height of hills of challenge varies,
The view appears complex,
As my future hides behind diffused perspex.

Facing the stigma of restricted mobility.
Facing barriers constantly.
Facing suffering in beds of sickness,
Made by Society.
Sharing drops of experience,
Slowly learning acceptance.

Marilyn Longstaff
ENGLAND

Marilyn's work has appeared in a number of magazines, anthologies and on the web, and she is currently a member of the writing, performing and publishing collective Vane Women. In 2003, Marilyn received a Northern Promise Award from New Writing North, and in 2005 gained her MA in Creative Writing from the University of Newcastle. She has written five books of poetry and, in 2011, her book *Raiment* (Smokestack Books) was selected for New Writing North's Read Regional campaign. The poems for her latest pamphlet, *The Museum of Spare Parts* (2018 Mudfog), came from her involvement in *Stemistry*, a University of Newcastle Public Engagement project, devised and run by Lisa Matthews, to consider creative responses to modern genomics. Her other books are: *Puritan Games* (Vane Women Press, 2001), *Sitting Among The Hoppers* (Arrowhead Press, 2004) and *Articles of War* (Smokestack Books, 2017).
E: marilynclong@aol.com

HERON

Uncomfortable in his shape, he hated
the weight of himself, that he could break
her wrist with an affectionate squeeze.

But height was his real burden. He walked
with his head hunched into his neck, to try
to make himself look shorter.

All this did was draw attention to his legs.
Is the air a bit thin up there? complete strangers
would joke; couldn't fathom why he didn't find this funny.

Always, he tried to hide his size 16 feet,
under a chair, behind a table. Paddling
was good – he could sink a few inches.

He sweated a lot. A fine sheen
on his brow made him look varnished.
No-one knew where he'd come from –

an oval peg in a round hole – his Dad
was five foot four, his Mum smaller. He was taller
than his brothers, school friends, work mates –

head and shoulders. He wore a lot of grey
to try to blend into the background.
Asked himself, often, what she saw in him.

Previously published in *Raiment* (Smokestack Books, 2010).

STREET IN SAMOIS
After the painting by Odilon Redon (1888).

Once, in this deserted street –

>a short street of golden stone
>that draws you in to its vanishing point;
>houses that conjure cosy, homely, warm,
>that promise interiors of workers,
>and their families eating, drinking,
>chatting at the kitchen table, houses
>that turn their backs on the outside silence –

Redon sketched a boy
carrying a heavy bundle of sticks,
weighed down in midday heat
labouring up the sandy road.

But now, as he and his wife
mourn the loss of their first child, Jean,
Redon removes the lad and his burden
from the final painting.

Previously published in *Articles of War* (Smokestack Books, 2017).

S. D. Kilmer

NEW YORK, USA

S. D. Kilmer is a retired Existential/Pastoral Therapist, Pastoral Care Specialist and Family Conflict Mediator, and has been writing poetry since 1968. He has been published online in *Stillwords* (2021), in the anthology *Manchester and beyond* (2020), with two poems in the forthcoming anthology *Around the World* (2022).
E: heardwordsllc@gmail.com
W: www.SDKilmer.com

IS THERE NOTHING MORE?

Dinner is on the wall
Children crying, infant screaming
Fear freezes her when he calls
Between them there is silence peeling
Its the way they only know
Its how love they struggle to show
He knows nothing more
She can't bear the blood and sores
She understands she must flea
But how else can she Be?

DISTRACTED LIVING

Blue Light fills your eyes
Digital noise deafens your soul
Your body can't process the processed foods you consume.
There's no time to sleep
You let it all pass you by.
While in this cyber world
Without any introspection you will never cry.
You are lost to yourself.
Your moods, your emotional direction
Your very existence now
Here, dictated by electronic information
I never got the chance to say to you,
Goodbye.

HE WAS ALWAYS YOURS

Mother Susan, how did you cope?
Did you have a smoke of rope?
That day, February 25, 1988
You could have bathed your child
In your tears.
So infectious was your sorrow.
I began to wish for tomorrow
The child could be ours, instead.
Yours and mine.
Adoptive father and birthmother.
Only I can think like no other.
I followed your career.
So similar to my own.
A Counsellor of Compassion.
Continued to wish Anthony be ours.
As the hours sifted, swayed.
Time slipped away.
My marriage went from farce to divorce.
What other direction of course?
I always hoped I might present
Our son back to you.
Facilitate the Mother and Child reunion.
But Anthony found you, I hear.
Without me.
He disowned me, and the other.
Did he say how I was as a Father?
Oh Susan.
I guess he could never have been ours.
He was always yours.

*Anthony (given name) Nathaniel (adoptive name).
**The author is both an Adoptee & an Adoptive Father.

Donna Zephrine
NEW YORK, USA

Donna was born in Harlem, New York and grew up in Bay Shore, Long island. She graduated from Columbia University School of Social Work in May 2017, and currently works for the New York State Office of Mental Health at Pilgrim Psychiatric Center Outpatient SOCR (State Operated Community Residence). She is a combat veteran who completed two tours in Iraq. She was on active duty army, stationed at Hunter Army Airfield 3rd infantry Division as a mechanic. Since returning home, Donna enjoys sharing her experiences and storytelling through writing. Donna's stories most recently have been published in *New York Times, On The Road, War and Battle, The Seasons, Qutub Minar Review, Bards Initiative, Radvocate, Oberon, Long Island Poetry Association* and *The Mighty*.
E: kauldonna@yahoo.com
FB: @donna.zephrine
Twitter: @dzephrine
Instagram: @donnazephrine
LinkenIn: @donna-zephrine-30300636

EDUCATIONAL STRUGGLES

A little girl label with learning disabilities
struggled in grade school.
frustrated keeping up with her peers
she still had a desire to learn
even though the process took longer
The Junior ROTC program
Provided discipline for her to move on
She graduated high school
and went on to college.
Had a little difficulty transitioning from high school to college.
Now that little girl with learning disabilities
Has earned her bachelor's and master's degree

Nivedita Karthik
INDIA

Nivedita is a graduate in Immunology from the University of Oxford. She is an accomplished Bharatanatyam dancer and published poet. She also loves writing stories. Her poetry has appeared in *Glomag, The Society of Classical Poets, The Epoch Times, The Bamboo Hut, Eskimopie, The Sequoyah Cherokee River Journal, The Ekphrastic Review,* and *Visual Verse.* Nivedita also regularly contributes to the open mics organized by Rattle Poetry. She currently resides in Gurgaon, and works as a scientific and medical editor/reviewer.
E: nivedita5.karthik@gmail.com
W: www. justrandomwithnk.com
YouTube: @JustrandomwithNK

THE SEASONS OF ADVERSITY

Summer
The dog days of summer are here to stay
with their humid showers and blistering heat rays.
Yet a cool glimmer of hope beckons us to move on
for it will be autumn this coming dawn.

Autumn
The piercing winds of autumn rattle our teeth
while a carpet of red and gold crackles beneath our feet.
Yet the warmth of a blazing hearth beckons us to move on
for it will be winter this coming dawn.

Winter
The season of shivery discontent is now going strong
poking and prodding to get us to move on along.
Yet, sluggishly we move till a thought galvanizes our mind
If winter comes, can spring be far behind?

Spring
Although remnant chills momentarily stop us in our tracks,
at no time thus far did adversity decide to drop its axe.
And now, finally, this new season showers us with hope
giving us the strength to navigate wisely adversity's tricky jump rope.

ADVERSITY NO MORE

The icy heart also breaks when facing adversity,
but the shards form a cavern, enclosing the warm red blood that
flows beneath.
     What an oxymoron
Protected and safe, the blood pulses and pounds its way
till it melts the cavern that protected it
and gushes out
in an outpouring at once silent and strong
that adversity stands no chance at all.

ADVERSITY IS

Adversity is the 'gigantic' hill
with jagged rocks and slippery slopes.
Yet, climb it we must till
we reach the peak and feel the miracle of hope.

Adversity is the deep 'black' sea
where no light shines through.
Yet, swim we must till we see
the glints of gold shining through the blue.

Adversity is the deep and narrow vale
with the peaks of hope far above.
Yet, navigate it we must on our own trail
carved out with determination and love.

Kakoli Ghosh
INDIA

Kakoli Ghosh (a.k.a. Moon Drops) is a post-graduate in English literature. She is a multilingual writer: many of her poems in vernacular Bengali language have been published online and in local magazines. She has self-published a poetry book titled *Unfinished from Durban, South Africa,* and one of her poems, *Grains of Salt*, was published in a South African anthology *Poems for Haiti*. Her work has been published in various anthologies including: *Paradise on Earth: Vols. I & II, Ferring Love,* and *Glomag.*
E: kakolimajumdarghosh@gmail.com
FB: @moon.drops.773
Instagram: @moondrops_2020

LIGHT OUTLIVES FIRE

Patience endures the blaze of violence,
Thunder slits the dark in flashes bright.
But it has its brevity of significance,
Tiny sparks can't flame mellowed light.
Wings of flight scorch in fatuous glory,
Ignited tomorrows sizzle like embers;
Fatigued fumes of pride rains ordinary,
Tolerance left in silver ash smoulders.

Choked dreams murmur in dry leaves,
Pregnant corpses breed bloody peace.
Brewed life strain through rusty sieves,
Flooding terror stagnate and freeze .
Tongue of thunder stammers in anger,
Washed in a shower, light outlives fire.

BLOOMING WOUNDS

Are you bewildered to see
my wounds blooming !
See how the deep sores of adversity
swathed in love, has started to heal,
and the leaking pride of death, seal !

Look at the desperate blood
that had gushed out once like flood,
now choking the birth canal of the sun
with wads of gunpowder clods;
from heaven unheard prayers return.

Leaning on each other's shoulder
success and failure share a lit cigar
in between their confident fingers.
Trudging through the remnants of war
they stumble on the rubbles of power.

Fatigued graves gently smother
the wind pipe of violence and terror.
Burning and fuming patience, raped,
gives birth to another naked sun.
Breath meets life at a sudden turn.

SPIDER

Trapped in its own thick web
the shocked spider,
writhing and wiggling
in the sticky net of its own desire
feels insecure and goes haywire.

Entangled as a poisonous gesture
it suffers a throbbing death
that never do expire;
the dark mildewed corners
shelter and suspend its cold breath.

The woven spit of its tension
hanging in the smoky mesh
of fear and protection,
imprisons its own delight.
His unsure limbs creep in sooty light.

The cleaner's sweeping bash
wraps up its outstretched trash
from the corners of doubt and misery;
the drowsy cobwebs are forgotten,
sunken eyes of depravity sleep rotten.

Bill Cushing
CALIFORNIA, USA

Bill lived in several states, the Virgin Islands, and Puerto Rico before moving to California. He earned an MFA in writing from Goddard College in Vermont, and now lives in Glendale with his wife and their son. Along with writing and facilitating a writing group (9 Bridges), Bill's book of poems, *A Former Life*, was released by Finishing Line Press and was recently honoured with a Kops-Featherling International Book Award. Published in various journals and anthologies worldwide, both in print and online, he is a multiple Pushcart Prize nominee, and was named among the Top Ten L.A. Poets in 2017, as well as one of 2018's "ten poets to watch" by Spectrum Publishing of Los Angeles, along with winning the 2019 San Gabriel Valley Chapbook Competition with *Music Speaks*, a volume republished and honoured by the 2021 New York City Book Awards.
E: piscespoet@yahoo.com

FATHER'S DAY: JUNE 20, 2004

I watched my mother die over days:
Eyes sealed shut, glazed
with a crust of time;
occasional sounds pantomiming
conversation; breathing
barely there and marked
with wearied effort.
Hands sprout
from two thin and shrivelled
arms laying
wherever placed; her legs,
scabbed from the falls
of her last
conscious moments.

My father, the martial stoic,
sits beside her,
leans into her, and
whispers in her ear,
"It's okay to go
if you wish," telling her,
"I'm ready."
In a half-century
of life,
I had never seen
such tenderness:
his age-mottled hands stroke
shallow cheeks,
a half-finger
brushes back brittle hair,

and while it took three days to complete -
on this Father's Day, my father inclined
to give my mother
the gift of dying.

First published in *A Former Life* (Finishing Line Press, 2019).

GABRIEL'S COMING

Things did not turn out
as perfectly as we had hoped. When
the doctors
extracted him
from the womb, there he was

a twisted pretzel of
a person, this child
who was
to be
perfect,
shaking and bloody
as a wounded bird and
not much different:

from the bony shoulders, like broken wings,
crooked arms splayed up
to the curled hands
that seemed jammed
under a quivering
chin
attached, haphazardly,
to a crooked head.

Hips
perpendicular to
a withered torso,
legs running
up the sides of a pruney chest —

all these deformities
from blood that had
clotted in the brain:
a stroke. So,
a malady
of the elderly became
his personal anomaly.
Blood soaked, crooked,
crying, and
brain damaged:
this was how we greeted
our son,

yet
from those bodily barricades
and
out of that
unquenchable panic
came
a boy who
      did not interrupt a family,
      did not join a family,
but who
created a family.

First published in *A Former Life* (Finishing Line Press, 2019).

Rachel Elion Baird
MASSACHUSETTS, USA

Raised on the pabulum of the west coast literary and art renaissance, Rachel is a member of the Edinburgh School of Poets, and the author of two published poetry collections: *Uplands*, and *Valentines and other Tragedies*. She is a writer, artist, poet and singer/songwriter, whose work appears in numerous publications including *New Millennium Writings, South Light, Deluge Journal* and *Into the Void,* as well as in experimental film and multimedia installations. Offering up poetry as a language of shared experience, Rachel's poems are confessional, intentionally accessible and often visual, unfolding stories through descriptive imagery.

E: rachelbaird9@gmail.com
W: www.rachelelionbaird.com
Instagram: @weather.girl1000
Twitter: @rachelbaird1122

TWO OF EARTH

Driving down empty streets
to check my mail again.
I am not expecting much,
just hoping for something to appear,
and there it is, a letter
posted two months ago – yours.
You are alone, catching up on things
mundane and fantastical,
living off what grows – gathering
on an island off an island
off yet another island –
how we all are these days.

I will write back soon
about the wild creatures
used to me by now – we watch each other,
how the mist visits most mornings,
leaves after breakfast is done,
and my pepper grinder
is snowing coal, leaving swaths
like those sweeping black rivers
of iron ore dust,
etch-a-sketch
on the beach where you grew up.

First published in *Portraits from a Pandemic.*

THREE OF EARTH

You were imagining your future –
all the thoughts, events,
yours and mine,
caught up in a life,
the what-if you could guide
your chariot, sure handed?
Which way to turn, to see
what was on the road
farther ahead?
Knowing the way love and hate
can strangely go hand-in-hand,
your brain whispers a memory,
how change is always possible –
second, even third chances,
blue skies and salt boxes,
to hold on, walk these lands
together, with the hope of it all
not forgotten,
222 days and counting,
alone, alone.

First published in *Portraits from a Pandemic.*

EIGHT OF EARTH

So many changes
and I can feel myself
changing too,
I follow the trail in fits and starts,
becoming round – turning
like a wheel
going this way and that.

Finally, deciding to wait it out,
hold-up with Temperance,
her wings folded earthward,
wading through the middle way
to clear waters and solid ground,
somewhere,
there must be.

First published in *Portraits from a Pandemic.*

Brajesh Singh
INDIA

Brajesh is a writer, poet and translator, and completed his Postgraduate from Lucknow University, India. His poems appeared in the international anthology *Ancient Egyptians, Modern Poets* and in a number of online magazines and journals including *Atunis Galaxy Poetry*. His Hindi articles, poems, and translations have been published in *Sahitya Kunj, Hastakshar*, and daily newspapers, and he is a member of the editorial team of the Kritya International Poetry Festival.
E: bsingh.idup@gmail.com
FB @Brajesh Singh

A TORCH

(I)
Me, a flickering torch,
to whom shown a path,
same are waiting feverishly
for my last breath.

(II)
Me, a flickering torch
who illuminated everything faraway,
but now regretting myself,
that couldn't enlighten the torchbearer
suffering from envy,
and under his mighty palm, to herself.

(III)
Me, a torch,
in soft hand of a child
at picturesque valleys of Manali.

An afternoon
warns tourists for everyone's future,
the churn of the third tsunami,
may take away
our gleeful laughter,
colourful dreams, innocent faces,
songs echoing in twilight,
flourishing fields, swaying beaches
tsunami is ready
to swallow everything.

So, Live and let live
listen to his gentle warning,
where is your mask?

(IV)
A flickering torch,
just now lit many pyres at riverside
and streamed silent lamentations.

Dimming light of crematorium,
water mirror reflected the scorched polymorph
wearing a mask with poisonous laughter.

Nicknamed in the Roman alphabet,
erasing all other languages and dialects,
as if self-declaration of the universal king of skeletons.

Suddenly! a spark fell on the water mirror,
impregnable fortress began to collapse
and animalistic laughter follows.

(V)
Beaches waving with laughter,
resonating valleys with songs,
alive colourful nights, dazzling lively stadiums,
some prisoners just released from jails
and gatherings inviting Tsunami.

A fake global emperor with an ugly face
wearing a subtly spiky crown, with the genetics of SARS-COV-2,
by mutations in nucleotide and RNA genome
transformed in archenemy of human being
as soon Genealogy defines, each variant is nicknamed.

Alpha, Beta, Gamma, Delta
Eta, Iota, Kappa and Lambda,
Greek alphabet neither to learn
nor to solve calculations of geometry;
just an awakening of his transmission.

Renowned virologist world over
putting their best to invent Brahmastra in laboratories
for modern Raktbeej variants,
lethal demons penetrating
the thorax of angels along with all of us.

The torch warns
Vaccinate everyone, the distance of two yards,
Facemask and hand sanitization are musts.

NOTE:
Brahmastra - a mythological infallible weapon
Raktbeej- a mythological demon defeated by Goddess Kali

First published by *Atunis Galaxy Poetry* (September, 2021).

Kate Young
ENGLAND

Kate is semi-retired and lives in Kent. She is a teacher and has been passionate about poetry since childhood. With a love of art, Kate writes a lot of Ekphrastic poetry, and enjoys visiting galleries for inspiration. She also loves reading, dancing, painting, and playing the guitar and ukulele, and belongs to three poetry groups which have helped and supported her in recent years. Her poems have appeared in *Ninemuses, Ekphrastic Review, Nitrogen House, The Poetry Village, Words for the Wild, Poetry on the Lake, Alchemy Spoon* and two Scottish Writers Centre chapbooks. Her work has also featured in the anthologies *Places of Poetry* and *Write Out Loud*. Her pamphlet *A Spark in the Darkness* won The Baker's Dozen competition with Hedgehog Press, and is due to be published. Her poem *The Last Stars* was shortlisted in The Poetry on the Lake Competition 2021.
E: kateyoung12@hotmail.co.uk
Twitter: @Kateyoung12poet.

SCALING NEVIS

Impossible, the doubters claim.
Impossible, your body screams
as you plant your foot in cloud-break
each etch and crag of granite on Nevis
worn into your skin like a canker.

You breathe in the roll of haar,
its rise and fall kissing the backs
of sleeping giants clothed in risk
and the slow unspool begins.

Delete the smile, exhale the air,
uproot boot from scrag of peak,
plant it firmly on saddle behind,
perilous back-step, disengage.

Weaken the sun as hours rewind,
re-absorb sweat, downclimb time
to basecamp, untie knot on boot,
back-climb in car, ignition re-start.

Reverse up strath, re-park in bay,
moonwalk corridor, re-close door,
un-plunge syringe, de-tube the vein,
retreat from ward, forward time.

A splitter of a smile cracks the North Face
your pride lighting the summit at dusk,

scale the impossible, ascend.

A MOTHER'S LOVE

Aleppo tastes of dust.
It smothers the woman's tongue
in a swallow of hate.

The streets reek of filth,
of crumbled brick and anguish
the colour of despair.

She squats, low as a cockroach
hidden in a crevice and waits.
Fear radiates in light,

a crackle of shells ricochet,
whistle through acrid air
and rattle through alley-dirt.

Her eyelids close,
shutter out ancient citadels
of long-lost civilisations

now clothed in rumbled ash,
the rub of ruin fragile
as the boot-weary stone.

A thin whimper vibrates on skin,
and she folds her arms
around him, cradles him.

A mother's love is everything.

ANSWERS ON THE BACK OF A POSTCARD PLEASE

While some mothers sifted flour into cakes,
ours sifted debt through shaky fingers
like the random shuffle of overdue bills
into piles of paper on cracked Formica,
in the vague hope that final demands
would be lost in the middle of the pack.

She rifled through competitions
in that cramped, damp little space
we called home. Naively, she believed
that answers on the back of a postcard
might erase problems more complex
than a missing puzzle piece could solve.

Back then, Friday night was 'Collection Night'.
Fingers scrabbled for crosses on coupon,
scraping together small change of fortune
before The Pools' Man appeared in corduroy,
impatient feet, a soft-shuffle on doorstep
like a windfall of leaves in autumn.

Odds on it was the usual crash
of fist on glass that brought weekend
stumbling in, Our Steve having spent wages
on vodka, cheap as chips,
from local offie, expecting
to find answers on the insides of bottles.

In later years Mam played the lottery
with dogged optimism. She chanced her luck
to wash stains and smudges of despair
from walls where he once threw plates,
his rage spinning like a roulette wheel,
numbers blurred in a mishmash of risk.

Bill Cox
SCOTLAND

Bill was born and bred in 'the Granite City' of Aberdeen, Scotland and he currently lives there with his partner Hilary, and their grown-up baby daughter Catherine. Bill enjoyed creative writing when at school, but as the cliché goes, life got in the way and it was only in his forties, after taking an online course, that he returned to his teenage passion. He now writes for the sheer enjoyment of it, which is just as well as no-one seems willing to pay him to do it. He dabbles mainly in poetry and short fiction, as he hasn't built up the stamina yet to write anything longer. One day, though, he plans to gather his strength and write a book that will set the publishing world alight. In the meantime he satisfies himself with composing bawdy limericks in his head.
E: malphesius@yahoo.com
W: www.northeastnotesblog.wordpress.com

ADVERSITY: A HERO RISES

In times of calamity,
When fear burns strong,
And hope shatters into a thousand tiny pieces,
From where shall our heroes arise?

Will they stride forth from Valhalla's Halls,
Or quest from the Elysian Fields?
Do our heroes live in majestic splendour,
In the Houses of the Gods?

Or should we look to mortal men,
Whose jaw-lines clench and muscles swell,
As they dance with danger,
Hoping for a Hollywood ending?

Do such beings really exist,
Outside the screens and pages,
Where we project our fantasies?

What if, just what if,
There are no enchanted hammers or magic spells,
No demi-gods striding earth's dark hills,
No impossible agents or forgotten soldiers,
Back for one last mission?

What if our heroes were just us,
In our everyday clothes living our ordinary lives?
No super powers, no witty quips,
Just doctors, nurses, checkout girls and boys,
Drivers, carers, teachers, husbands and wives,
All just doing their duty,
With that extra bit of care and attention.
Their only weapons are a cheerful word or reassuring smile,
That tell you that,
Even in the darkest of hours,
From a million different points,
The stars still brightly shine.

Vesna Mundishevska-Veljanovska

REPUBLIC OF NORTH MACEDONIA

Vesna is a member of the Macedonian Writers' Association, Macedonian Science Society – Bitola, and Bitola's Literary Circle. She is the author of thirteen books of poetry, two books of critical-essay texts, co-author of a book of poems for children and (co)author of six vocational books for teachers. Her poetry has been translated into many languages, awarded and represented in anthologies. She is editor of the Journal of Culture – Literature, Drama, Film and Publishing – *Sovremeni dijalozi/ Contemporary Dialogues*, editor-in-chief of two magazines for students, and a member of the Macedonian Science Society' Ethics Committee. She was editor of the Journal of Literature, Art and Culture *Rast/Growth*, editor-in-chief of the journal *Sovremeni dijalozi/ Contemporary Dialogues*, editor and editor-in-chief of the literary bulletins *Plima* and *Izrek*, editor of the Journal for modern education and science *Vospitni krstopati/ Educational Crossroads*, and editor of the bulletin for teachers *Razgledi*. She has also edited forty poetry books and collections. She was president of the Literature and Culture Association 'Razvitok,' and of the Literary Youth of Macedonia – Bitola, as well as secretary of the writers' association Bitola's Literary Circle. She is Ambassador of Peace in Cercle Universel Des Ambassadeurs De La Paix - Suisse/France.

E: vesnamv13@yahoo.com

GLIMPSE

Translated from Macedonian into English by Vesna Mundishevska-Veljanovska.

My cornea crumbles
memories from the lake shore
and murmur of shells
white flashed like snow.

Only the selectiveness of a flock of seagulls
peeps in this morning's frames,
and also the inventiveness of five to six children
for playing fish and frog games.

Now the calm water
is hiding inside itself,
and the mud soaks
the loneliness of a handful of stones.

The requiem of algae
vibrates in solitude,
and the lakescape is hypnotized
by a little snake's hip-hop mood.

A man who was measuring
both the beauty and asperity of shallowness
struck with a stone, as a lightning testimony,
and interrupted this polyphony.

At the incision of the moment
even the time spasmed.

Did the curious crush
serpent's evil endowment
or did he kill our prejudices!?

These in-mind stresses
will be my know-how
for what I was
and
what I am now.

Gabriella Garofalo
ITALY

Born in Italy some decades ago, at age just six, Gabriella both fell in love with the English language and started writing poems in Italian She has contributed to a number of national and international magazines and anthologies, and is the author of *Lo sguardo di Orfeo, L'inverno di vetro, Di altre stelle polari, Casa di erba, Blue branches* and *A Blue Soul*.
E: grrz2001@yahoo.it

I CAN'T REACH YOU

I can't reach you, my waves, you are flying too high,
And I'm stuck on a balcony, a dog-end in my hand,
While chavs in tracksuits get sloshed
On cheap lager or alcopops,
Those sudsy dramas everyone and their mother
Seems to go nuts over -
Sure, Orpheus' lyre may come in handy,
Or is it rotting in the grass
While our limbs are stretching out to eternity?
Look, once we sang weird songs,
Maybe out of key, but would always play
Charming tunes, right?
But don't spin it nice, you know she was living
Under ambush and siege, that old pit in the yard,
And rotten icy water, the impotence
You drink whenever sand and waves
Snag your mind that's fading
Like a winter sunset, cold or distant-
Stop it now, she's just dashing out
To flowers, to fruits, to an impossible end,
Words, maybe demise -
So, don't swear against the light,
It's just some rhyming words,
Don't strand the paths mothers define
To snuff out fathers and secluded limbs-
Go on my angels, catch some light, and store it
In the locker, words being our North Star
If you wander through mazes, or life,
And you get lost, my time, please swing-by
In unseen lands of light as she's showing off-
Long story short, don't spin it nice
If clouds shroud the sky, or ice splinters die:
C'mon, my soul, hit the road, darn all those red lights,
Hide among caves, boulders, who bloody cares
If you skid when blazing rows
With mantises or lunar midlands
Set you ablaze -
Yes, you, your life, your words carved
In an ancient idiom they never grasped -
Who? Your folks, of course, your friends, and time -
But no longer icy the stars will shelter your heaven,
In due time, and properly, as it should be-

By the way, who are those shapes peeking along?
Fake news as ever, or mornings
Painting the sky in garish blue?
Well, with a pinch of luck, you may call 'em angels -
Sure, why not? Is my Nisirine the bluest of them?

Tracy Davidson
ENGLAND

Tracy lives in Warwickshire, and writes poetry and flash fiction. Her work has appeared in various publications and anthologies including: *Poet's Market, Writing Magazine, Mslexia, Atlas Poetica, Modern Haiku, The Binnacle, A Hundred Gourds, Shooter, Artificium, The Garden, Journey to Crone, The Great Gatsby Anthology, WAR, In Protest: 150 Poems for Human Rights.*
E: james0309@btinternet.com

THE FORGOTTEN ONES

Orphans. Maimed ones. Not the pretty able-bodied ones
celebrities fly half-way round the world to adopt.
A little girl makes her way outside on makeshift crutches,
her left leg gone, right foot amputated, the leg
ending in a misshapen ugly stump.
It looks red and sore. She hasn't got used to the crutches yet,
and they're a little short, so her stump keeps bumping the ground.
Infection is likely to set in. She might lose more.

A teenage boy, so nearly – but not quite – a man, stares moodily
across the yard. Both legs gone, one arm hanging lifeless at his side.
He watches the other boys play football. Playing as best they can
with their various combinations of missing and mangled limbs,
one who's sightless but follows the ball through sound,
another with shrapnel lodged deep in his brain. It will work
its way through until it kills him. But he's smiling now
and whooping, daydreaming of the World Cup.

A charity worker comes to the door to watch, needing a break
from nursing those too sick to play.
She blinks back tears, trying to forget the baby boy,
just four months old, who died in her arms during the night.
She hasn't been here long enough to harden her heart
and accept that sometimes death is kinder.

An ambulance enters the compound, making her look up
and the children pause in their games.
Two stretchers are lifted out, the thin blood-soaked
blankets showing what parts are missing beneath.

The nurse sighs and calls to her colleagues, break over,
and wonders for the umpteenth time: "When will it end?"

First published: *In Protest: 150 Poems for Human Rights*, Human Rights Consortium, 2013.

FADE AWAY

I thought my heart would break that day
when the doctor told us the news.
I watched you fade and drift away.

He said the cancerous cells may
have spread, there was no time to lose.
I thought my heart would break that day.

The dread disease moved in to stay,
few treatment options left to choose.
I watched you fade and drift away.

And when your skin had turned to grey
you begged me feed you pills and booze.
I thought my heart would break that day.

We tried to keep your pain at bay,
a shell made up of bone and bruise.
I watched you fade and drift away.

At last, no demons left to slay,
hundreds of mourners filled the pews,
I thought my heart would break. That day
I watched you fade and drift away.

Cheryl-Iya Broadfoot
ENGLAND

Cheryl-Iya is an avid Soul Adventurer. Created and raised in Johannesburg, South Africa, she is now based in London. Her first adventures began in the classroom, daydreaming instead of learning, writing and poetry were always secret loves ... Chocolate and tea-lover, usually found helping women launch successful and sustainable businesses, she has been known to caress the realms of the typed-word occasionally (as a novice). She loves to follow her own soul's compass, and in doing so has found herself entertaining people with her short-stories and poems. She is self-published, twice, in self-help and a number of times in various anthologies. She is researching her third self-help book. On her journey she has met a host of writing-angels (human and celestial) all busy helping her grow her global snowball of happiness through as many means as possible, despite a number of health concerns. She carries on regardless, and enjoys it!
E: souls_compass@yahoo.com
W: www.wellbeingshowcase.com
W: www.soulscompass.net

I'LL HAVE TO TRY

What use is freedom, if I'm only free to choose
my chains?
If a flower sees no sun,
how can it share
joy and beauty …
In a prison of my own
making,
the walls keep moving,
taunting me with hope,
dangling an exit carrot-like.
Yet the sun never shines,
the seed lays buried
cold, alone, afraid,
waiting for conditions
to be right:
for liquid, for warmth,
for light.
And even if I bloom,
will I ever be free
from the depression
that rules me?
(I'll have to try).

BREATHE AGAIN

I learn to breathe again,
my lungs fill with fresh air.
The hospital ventilator
just a dream
that fades behind me.

I sit in my garden,
no longer imprisoned
by four walls
and masked medics.

A buzz of honey bees
instead of beeps
and hums of machines.
The sun warms my blood more
than any transfusion.

Birds sing to me, in between
trips to the bird feeder,
refilled once more.

Does the tame robin
still remember me?
How often I sketched him
in my mind
while too weak
to hold a pencil.

I will sketch him again.

For now, he hops
onto my hand
to feed from my fingers.

For now, we are both content,
each breath
a precious seed.

Shaswata Gangopadhyay
INDIA

Born and bought up in Kolkata, and graduating in Science and Corporate Management, Shaswata started writing poetry in the mid-'90s, and is now one of the prominent faces of contemporary Bengali poetry. Shaswata has exhibited at the Poetry Festival in Picollo Museum, Italy, and has participated in a large number of poetry festivals across Europe and the USA. His poetry has been published in all the major journals of Bengali literature, and has been translated into English and published in journals and anthologies in Europe, America, Asia, Africa and Latin America. His book of poems are: *Inhabitant of Pluto Planet* (2001), *Offspring of Monster* (2009) and *Holes of Red Crabs* (2015).
E: shaswatagangopadhyay@gmail.com
FB: @shaswata.gangopadhyay.7

A BALLAD ON ESTRANGEMENT

You're not easily available ,for me very tough to meet you
On the Nilgiri mountain, Kurinji flowers blooming
in autumn, every twelve years gap,
you resemble the very identical species

You've bloomed once again during this season, all over the valley
those suffering from leprosy, assemble there and believe that
they'll be cured if they paste grinding petals of
a rare species like you, on their wounds
all their old maladies'll be gone for good.
Following the equator, I've also come here
we are belonging to the same planet, but rarely meeting each other
I'll climb to search you, using the worn-out staircase through mist
will lie down tiringly on the notch of a stone, you just cast off upon
my body, open your petals from head to the fingers of your two legs
let the storm dash out, if you put your lips on my lips

You're the sanatorium to me, the secret panacea

Jill Sharon Kimmelman
DELAWARE, USA

Jill is a Pushcart Prize nominee. Her international publication credits include *Vita Brevis Press, Spillwords Press, Fine Lines Journal, Loveoffood.net, Poetic Musings Ezine, HeartBeats, an Anthology* (2021), *Scentsibility, an Anthology*, (2020), *Two Hearts, ILA Literary Magazine, Stab The Pomegranate* and multiple poetry videos from Sparrow Productions. Her first book *You Are The Poem*, a coffee table collection of poems and photos in b&w and colour, by Jill and her husband - a former professional photographer - is scheduled for release in November, 2021.

E: jskimmelman@icloud.com

HEALING MAGIC

This barrel of grief, once hollow, black
without floor or perch, frightens me a little less
with each rung of the climbing out

I am traveller gazing upon splendid vistas
a gift of lanterns light my way, opalescent pearls
and magic beads illuminate the pale dawn

When I stumble on unfamiliar roads, my dress is rimmed
with mystic dust
so I walk a little slower, no need to hurry this journey

Sweet temptation beckons beneath the invitation
of this stranger's welcome smile
I bend like a willow to show a fellow traveller
the grace of my limbs and the recognition in my eyes

This has the makings of healing magic.

Jane Fuller
SCOTLAND

Jane is a full time carer and occasional writer living on a cliff top in the South Rhins of Galloway, near Stranraer, Scotland. She has had poetry, flash fiction and short stories published in journals and curated web-zines as diverse as *Football Poets, The Linnet's Wings, Northwords Now, Writers Against Prejudice, I Am Not A Silent Poet* and *Writing in a Woman's Voice*. She has contributed to a range of community based projects such as 'Weed From A Drawing Wave,' an exploration of smuggling in the local area past, present and future funded by D&G Unlimited and *Undiscovered Treasures – New Writing Based on Old Objects in Stranraer Museum* funded by the Wigtown Book Company. Her writing is inspired by the Scottish landscape and the voiceless. For example, people with profound and multiple disabilities and unpaid carers who have suffered abandonment during the pandemic.
E: janeswan.fuller@outlook.com

FALSE PROPHET

In no time
you'll be back upon your feet
In no time
you'll be dancing once again
In no time
the mountain track will feel less steep
In no time
you'll stand tall against the rain

But time can't
tame the wilds of memory
And time won't
fill the fissures of the soul
Time never
finds that long-lost jigsaw piece
It fails to
take a shattered glass and make it whole

In time
your uncurled spine might take the strain
In time
you'll grow a hard, unblistered crust
In time
you'll find enough courage to say

Nothing can heal a ruptured heart
time only gifts a mask to make it look that way

ORDINARY EVEREST

Dawn breaks
turbulent night becomes turbulent day

feed, wash, toilet, dress
collect up gear
medicate, triple check
repeat

Trekking to base camp
takes up most of our energy
we sit in the perpetual shadow of the elevation

Dawn breaks
turbulent night becomes turbulent day

feed, wash, toilet, dress
collect up gear
medicate, triple check
repeat

This plateau is comfortable
but the far away summit beckons
We see the way forward strewn
with forgotten corpses - only the strong
are memorialised by the mountain.

Dawn Breaks
repeat

Hands and feet are numbed by the
reiteration of small movements
We lean into the gale
it pushes us back to the
beginning

Dawn breaks
repeat

We achieve a small summit
it shows the way forward
to another
then another

and another

Don't look back into the drop

Ian Cognitō
CANADA

Ian is a poet from Vancouver Island. He is the author of three collections of poetr: *Animusings, Much Adieu about Nothing*, and *flora, fauna & h. sapiens* (the latter two, co-authored with Pat Smekal). Ian recently produced and edited an anthology on the topic of ageing (again with Pat), *Old Bones & Battered Bookends* unites poets from across Canada to explore this lofty topic in poetic form. This autumn, Ian will publish *Interchange*, a poetry/prose exchange with Ontario prose writer Anne Marie Carson. He is the producer/artistic director of *15 Minutes of Infamy*, a word-craft cabaret based in Nanaimo, BC, and runs an independent publishing company Repartee Press. Ian's previous incarnations have included language instructor, child and youth care-worker, and mask maker/clown.

E: repartee@telus.net
FB: @Reparteepress

BLINK

I escort my 92-year-old mother
all hunched over her walker
as she crosses cautiously over the threshold
of this generic Starbucks franchise
and we are suddenly immersed
in a sea of youth
no one over the age of 25, I presume
no one, that is, but us two

how she stands out here
in this place
the only grey hair
in this whole crowd
the only one with any kind
of assistive device
the only person with these
age-related physical challenges

oh, she stands out all right
perhaps even, somewhat of a decoy
to camouflage my own advancing age
so I can taste a bit of invisibility while
she stands out all sore-thumb aged
in this sea of life potential
gently bobbing on ebb and flow
like some weathered old buoy
marking the spot, a long line
reaching downwards
to the very bottom of this life
anchored to a past
metres and metres
below the surface
of this moment here

two young women
still girls but for their
air of mannered maturity
look our way, try not
to look our way, try not
to take in this anomaly
this musty presence, in this place
my sweet, unassuming

ancient mom, Gwynneth
(hear the sweet cadence of her name)
[...]
perhaps, they cannot quite fathom
how this phantom presence
could represent a peek
into their own futures...
metres and metres beyond
this point they inhabit, on the line
they are still so buoyant
so fresh-faced
so newly painted and appointed

"It will come sooner than you think"
I want to warn them
but who am I
to shatter their illusions?

Adrienne Stevenson
CANADA

Adrienne is a retired forensic scientist. She writes poetry, fiction and creative non-fiction. Her poetry has been widely published in print and online journals and anthologies, most recently in the *BeZine, eucalyptus & rose, Roots & Wings vol.2, Red Wolf Editions, Planisphere Q, Black Bough Poetry, MacroMicroCosm, Page & Spine, Poetry and Covid, Jaden,* and *Still Point Arts Quarterly*. Her stories have won prizes in several competitions, and two have been published in *Byline*. When not writing, she tends a large garden.
E: adrienne@magma.ca
Twitter: @ajs4t

TEARS

You've been crying again
— I can almost see the tear
in your heart.
        Tears leak out
overflow through weary eyes
gaping holes in your face
that ooze out bitter drops.

I don't know how to comfort
your pain, without exposing
my own disconsolate grief.

Our world is, by turns, burning
and flooding—insufficient tears
to quench the fires, nor enough
bodies to dam the torrents.

Weep for what was, stand
adamant against the tide
each our private Cnut
powerless in the face
of disaster.

THE COMEDIAN

I am small for my age
my almost hairless body
gleams in moonlight
like polished ivory

my slender form
has not yet bloomed
into adolescent glory
though I have rage enough

to confront the bullies
in my school yard
I defuse their taunts
with self-deprecation

making others laugh
my sole talent
observing the ridiculous
and reflecting it back

on those monstrous ghouls
that haunt my locker
plague my school days
inform my humour

I grow beyond them
emerge from my chrysalis
take flight on strengthened wings
triumph in my natural milieu

graduate from class clown
to comedian

STATUE

long days have seen you on your pedestal
clothed in outmoded dress and form
standing still, arm raised in triumph
the other resting on your horse
both of you in copper-rich bronze
long weathered into green
streaked and rimmed with pigeon dung

your days as emblem of your regime
— regretted and unmourned —
are numbered, as opponents rise
to throw you down, obliterate your evil
still your voice, relegate you to a museum
where your deeds will be exposed
in ways you never dreamed

still, there are those who applaud
your narrow, small-minded views
struggle to maintain their privilege
resist with all their moneyed might
the flow of time that will force
their demise — their acts unforgotten
so they will not recur

Anamika Nandy
INDIA

Anamika hails from Digboi, Assam. By profession she is an educationist. She loves to write poems and to express her emotions in words, and enjoys working towards the development of a better society.
E: anamika.sweety1431@gmail.com

A GARDENER'S MIRAGE

Desire rolled down the cheeks,
Eyes aided to exude it.
No sweet sound poured into ears,
No jovial wish to illuminate the heart.

Watering other's sapling,
Tending with utmost care,
Showering immense love,
Seemed all so trifle!

Fruit of other's garden,
Can never be called own.
No right can be claimed,
Even for momentary delight.
Fruit is owned by the owner,
A mirage gifted to the gardener.

A childless woman only knows,
The intense agony she undergoes.
The day long wait goes in vain,
When no cherished voice comes to say,
"I wish you Happy Mother's Day."

Wilda Morris
ILLINOIS, USA

Wilda is the Workshop Chair of Poets and Patrons of Chicago, and a past President of the Illinois State Poetry Society. She has published over 700 poems in anthologies, webzines, and print publications, including *The Ocotillo Review, Pangolin Review, Poetry Sky, Whitefish Review, Quill & Parchment* (for which she was the featured poet for November 2020), and *Journal of Modern Poetry*. For three years she chaired the Stevens Poetry Manuscript Competition. She has won awards for formal and free verse and haiku, including the 2019 Founders' Award from the National Federation of State Poetry Societies. Much of the work on her second poetry book, *Pequod Poems: Gamming with Moby-Dick* (published in 2019), was written during a Writer's Residency on Martha's Vineyard. For fifteen years, she has moderated a monthly poetry reading at Brewed Awakening Coffeeshop in Westmont, Illinois. A retired educator, she is working on a book of poetry inspired by books and articles on scientific topics. Her blog features a monthly poetry competition.
E: wem@ameritech.net
Blog: www.wildamorris.blogspot.com

IDENTITY

So this is what it all comes down to
at last. Half a small room. Not knowing
where I am or why. Pills, blood tests.
A few pictures on the bulletin board of people
I don't recognize. A giant teddy bear
which came from somewhere.
A roommate whose name I can't recall,
her TV blaring out words I can't understand.
Food I can't taste and don't want to eat;
someone commanding me to drink milk,
water, anything. A bouquet of flowers
from someone who says she loves me.
Strangers lifting me onto the commode,
fussing about which one will hold me up
while the other one wipes my butt.
What did you say my name is?

JULY: FOR FLORRIE
Beginning with a line by Lance Larson

The avalanche behind my breast bone
is a mixture of memory, grief and guilt.
The anniversary of your death passed
without a word of consolation from me,
my annual insensitivity to your parents' pain.
I only want to recall your birthday,
your laugh so alive, tinkling like wind chimes
in a summer breeze, or the clear notes of the bells
we played. I held your palsied hand,
helped you strike the red ball on the plastic stick
against rainbow-coloured chimes.
We made our own music, loving life despite its limits.
When your time came, you must have loved
death for its release from the chrysalis
in which your arms and legs were crushed.
Each summer I should arc caring words
across an early July sky, try to ease
the ache in your mother's heart.
I should celebrate the day you hatched
into a butterfly, and flew away,
free.

AFTER THE DEATH OF A GRANDCHILD
Beginning with a line by Mary Oliver

Maybe the cats are sound asleep. Maybe not.
Maybe there are mice in the basement.
looking for something to feed their young,
Perhaps the beagle is barking at the neighbour
walking his greyhound around the block.
Whatever. Does it matter? Do I care?

Maybe the coffee brewed as scheduled. Maybe not.
Maybe the phone is off the hook and a thousand
e-mails sit unanswered in the inbox.
Perhaps the clock radio came on, broadcasting
news of an earthquake, a flood, a fiery speech.
Whatever. Does it matter? Do I care?

Maybe it is sleeting or snowing. Maybe not.
Maybe the earth quit rotating on its axis,
and wobbled out of its orbit around the sun.
Perhaps all the stars have gone cold
and all the planets blinked out their lights.
Whatever. Does it matter? Do I care?

Maybe I am all alone in the house. Maybe not.
Maybe I hear the sound of small feet tripping
down the carpeted hallway toward my room.
Perhaps a small child creeps to my bedside,
crawls up beside me, puts arms around my neck.
It does matter. I do care.

Kathleen Bleakley
AUSTRALIA

Kathleen lives in Wollongong, on the south coast of eastern Australia. She has five published poetry & prose collections: *Letters,* (a Pocket Poet, 2020), *Azure* (a Pocket Poet, 2017), *Lightseekers,* photography by 'pling (2015), *jumping out of cars*, with Andrea Gawthorne, images by 'pling, (2004), and *Passionfruit & Other Pieces*, with prints by Hannah Parker (1995). Kathleen's poetry has been widely published in literary journals, including internationally.
E: leenimyy@gmail.com

TWO HEARTS
For 'pling

my heart beats
way too loud
breathing short & fast
waking at midnight
from deepest sleep

my heart beats
discordantly
i remember dr liz saying
a little arrhythmia
occasionally, is normal - fine

my heart beats
remembering plan e
you saying it's time
to ring dr who
gentle zen smile
time travelled
too fast
even for dr who
no generator
reached you

28 november 2018
i wake, custodian
of your quiet heart

First published in *Milestones* (Ginninderra Press, 2021).

John Laue

CALIFORNIA, USA

John is a teacher/counsellor, and a former editor of *Transfer, San Francisco Review* and *Monterey Poetry Review.* He has won awards for his writing including the Ina Coolbrith Poetry Prize at The University of California, Berkeley. With five published poetry books, the last *A Confluence of Voices Revisited* (Futurecycle Press), and a book of prose advice for people with psychiatric diagnoses (*The Columns of Joel Mobius*), he presently coordinates the reading series of The Monterey Bay Poetry Consortium.

E: Joelmobius@aol.com

THE THINKER

Beside the sidewalk
slanting up to the Hotel Lanai
are two cement benches.
Today a red-haired man
sits down on one
precisely in the pose
of Rodin's Thinker.
I watch him closely, curious,
for more than ten minutes.
Then the clock strikes twelve;
the hotel opens up
its dining room.
He rises and enters
with me still wondering:
Was he pondering
man's perilous existence;
composing symphonies;
replaying world-class matches;
planning buildings
which would revolutionize
our current architecture?
Or had he simply sat there
like a starving cat, thinking,
Food! Food! Food!

THE FRENZY
"There's a sucker born every minute." P. T. Barnum

In the sixth or seventh great hotel
we visit on Maui (We never stay there
but we like to look)

there's a pool, or rather a small lake,
round except for one large lava boulder
where staff members stand to feed the fish.

If you could only see these koi,
hundreds upon hundreds, of all sizes,
some pure gold, gleaming in the light,

some black velvet and albino white,
some yellow as the sun itself,
others variegated like collages.

Though signs prohibit feeding them,
a grinning man dressed in expensive silk
stands on the rock and gestures wide

as if to throw them tidbits.
A hundred hungry koi crowd in front of him,
rolling over one another in their frenzy.

I think of politicians' slick campaign talk,
"I'll make your lives O so much better
if you'll only vote for me!"

And the people, desperate for hope
put trust in him and his glib promises,
casting ballots for his programs.

Then the reversal comes,
the explanations in pure doubletalk,
the stony silence, the ignoring,

or complete abandonment as with this man
who, tiring finally of the fish,
steps jauntily off the rock,

and enters the hotel's exclusive dining room

where he can feast on fare
intended for the very rich,

drink the world's best wines,
and think up more amusing schemes
to pass his endless afternoons.

Vernes Subašić
BOSNIA AND HERZEGOVINA

Vernes has a master's degree in Bosnian/Croatian/Serbian language and literature. He writes poetry and prose. So far he has received three awards for his literary prose and the prestigious Mak Dizdar award for the best upcoming poet in Bosnia and Herzegovina. He has published a collection of poems titled *Papagaj sloboda,* and his stories and poems have been published in a number of regional literary magazines.

E: vernes.sub@gmail.com
FB: @vernes.subasic

PAINTING OVER

Trenches are dug deep
into the painter's face.
Tiny soldiers duck
to avoid the drops of sweat.

By the landscape of his forehead
he's his father's age.

*

My father's never told me of the battlefield.
I was finding the trenches and the arrangement
of the mine fields on the map of his face.

I eavesdropped on the stories:
I worked in the Medical Corps
collecting in my palms
the scattered brains of my friends.

*

The white paint covers the yellow stains on the wall.
He comes down the ladder, dips in the roller,
Wipes the salty drops off his brow:
If he hadn't bent down to grab his bag that day,
his spinal fluid would have spilled.
Next to him sat (some)buddy.

*

Is this enough for him
to be forgiven?

***

The bucket that once contained the white paint
I dragged from the spring
that year when the taps ran dry
and I was but a boy.

My mum needed it for laundry.

Back then missiles rained down
and one fell on the bridge
which I had to cross carrying the bucket.

It stuck like a dart on the board.
If it had gone off, the water would've surely spilled.

*

Is this a reason enough,
my children of one and three,
for forgiveness?

Paula Bonnell

MASSACHUSETTS, USA

Paula's poems have appeared and are forthcoming widely in the U.S. (*The American Poetry Review, Rattle, Spillway* & more), as well as accepted and published in Canada, England, India and Australia, and have won awards from Poet Lore, Negative Capability, the New England Poetry Club, and the City of Boston. She is a PEN New England Discovery writer, and won a PEN Syndicated Fiction Project Award for a short story. She has also reviewed books of poetry and fiction in major American newspapers and in literary magazines.
E: paulabonnell@gmail.com

CHANGING THE PAST

One of those things – like being
in two places at once – that probably violate the laws of
physics. Not a good idea
unless you want to risk implosion
or disappearing through the vanishing point or
whatever is the natural consequence of such a
violation. The laws of physics don't have to
be enforced; they simply state what's
inevitably going to happen under certain
conditions. They describe, not prescribe.
But just for a moment let's
consider that when you said, "You can't
possibly meet respectable people this way."
(through an ad in an alternative newspaper)
I'd responded, "You mean you're not respectable?"
And for another moment, think also about your asking
"Are you a snob?" and my replying "What do you mean
by 'snob'?" or "Snobbery takes place in class societies,
like England or most universities.", where everyone
has a standing above and below others; they're ranked.
This is America; we're all equal."

And I really don't know if you intended to insult
me by your first question or why, if you believed
what you said, you had decided to place or respond
to an ad.
        I'll just put it down to lack of social graces. Or
maybe, taking into account what you told me later
about how late it was in life that you had
your first meaningful relationship, that you were
something of a solipsist, not particularly social.
        Nevertheless, despite this unpromising start and
the brevity of our companionship, something tried to
happen. I would say your (avowed) mind-body problem
got in the way. Since then each of us abides separately,
you relating extensively to the laws of physics,
I merely speculating.

Madhavi Tiwary
KINGDOM OF BAHRAIN / INDIA

Madhavi's first rendezvous with writing was at college where her scribblings - which she fondly called 'poems' - were proudly and regularly passed on to like-minded class mates. It then took a decade for her to pick up writing again with zeal and zest. As a result, in the past few years, she has written about fifty articles and editorial columns, and has written as many poems, many of which are still hatching in the warmth of her private closet.
E: madhavi.dwivedi@gmail.com

A LIFE AKA ADVERSITY

He lumbered past me
in that sprawling garden
in the centre of posh balconies
and snooty cat walkers.
Amidst the constant flash of Ferragamo shoes
and brawny structures,
his sagging shoulders declared defeat.
His dishevelled hair was
a deafening broadcast of a messed up life.
His empty glance reminded me
of that withered pebble
lying lonely under the hefty heap of washed away dirt.
His tousled shirt
got even more trampled
under the violent weight
of that blue ribboned employee badge -
hanging hopelessly from his creased neck.
His dragging steps groaned the routine rhythm
of drudgery and distress.

Did I just see adversity walk past me?

Ankita Patel
INDIA

Ankika resides in Mumbai, and is a US citizen. It's been a time of revival of passion for her; as a scientist her actions are left-brain dominated, so she has taken this opportunity to metamorphize, and activate and enhance her right-brain by indulging in some writing. It has been a therapeutic journey so far, and making her life a rather balanced chemical equation.

E: ankita@alumni.stanford.edu

STILL STANDING

Standing strong
from eons long
through the scorching sun
through the squalling storm
the lone tree
withstanding
the winds whistling with wrath
the thunder threatening torrentially
the lightning loaded with loathe
still standing

Standing tall
as my anchor
to stall
the storm of rancour

Swaying side to side
still standing
to protect my pride
from crumbling

Standing alone
as my guiding stone
to grow deep roots
bravely battling the brutes

Standing green
as a support
in times lean
fortifying the fort

Withered and worn
emotionally torn
heavy heart
soul preparing to depart

The lone tree
still standing
finally free
after delivering my soul to its landing

Janet Bi Li Chan
AUSTRALIA

Born in Hong Kong, Janet is a multi-disciplinary artist, poet and writer who now lives in Sydney, Australia. Having published widely as an award-winning academic researcher in sociology and criminal justice for many decades, she now devotes her time to making visual art, aural and textual poetry to explore her own history and issues of justice, truth and reconciliation. She has been granted art/writing residencies at the SEA Foundation (Tilburg, The Netherlands), Santa Fe Art Institute (NM, USA), Bundanon Trust (NSW, Australia) and Varuna House (Australia). Her art has been shown in various group and solo exhibitions (the most recent in 2021 and 2020 at the AIRspace Projects Gallery in Sydney). Her poetry has been published in *Visual Verse, The Poetry School* (*Soundtext Anthology*, edited by Antosh Wojcik) and the *Firstdraft Writers Program* (forthcoming 2021).
E: j.chan@unsw.edu.au
W: www.jbili.net

YOU LAUGH

After Simon Armitage's 'You're Beautiful.'

You laugh because your body is naturally ticklish.
I rage because I think good nature is a scarce
resource to be doled out judiciously.

You laugh because you open your heart to sunshine.
I rage because I feel seeing the storm ahead
is what a responsible adult does.

You laugh because you love that laughter is infectious.
I rage because the last time I tried to be funny
in a party I ended up with five enemies.

You laugh because so many things in the news are absurd.
I rage because I want to keep up the anger against
stupid ideas, not dilute it through ridicule.

You laugh because you appreciate the irony in the cartoon.
I rage because in my view no one has made
the world better by poking fun at politicians.

You laugh because you see the silver lining in dark events.
I rage because I believe in being prepared for
the worst, hoarding stuff during the pandemic.

You laugh because you are grateful for the cat's purring.
I rage because I reckon life is never going to be
a bed of roses; we had better get used to loneliness.

STATIONS OF THE CROSSED

The first was lying on the floor to stop feeling
faint, self-medicating
with folk remedies
until denial ran out of steam.

The second was subjecting to prescribed
jabbing of veins,
extraction of samples,
analysis of data haystacks.

The third was facing a sudden shift
of reality, showing up
at emergency, begging
for attention, a helpless patient.

The fourth was giving in to the web
of probes, consenting to
being wired to monitors,
welcoming transfusions.

The fifth was ignoring the noise
in the ward, moaning, retching,
grown-up crying, loudmouths
calling mates on their mobile.

The sixth was preparing for serious
Intervention, submitting
to deeper, longer probes
leading to a shocking diagnosis.

The seventh was packing the phone
charger, clothes, toothbrush,
signing up for an unknown
future in the hands of medicine.

The eighth was trying to remember how
to pray and to whom,
suppressing anger,
pushing a silent bargain.

The ninth was emerging from the fog
of anaesthetic, pumping fentanyl

for the pain, being woken
every hour to be tested.

The tenth was learning to walk
down the hall, dragging
a tangle of tubes attached
to bags hung on a pole on wheels.

The eleventh was finally being sent
home with a reformed body,
fresh wounds in bandages,
pain-killers on tap.

The twelfth was letting practicality
take over daily rituals,
making up ways of coping
with a different life.

The thirteenth was letting the body
find its peace, focusing
on freedom, even as
surveillance was a life sentence.

The fourteenth was refusing to meet
deadlines, attend Zoom
meetings, act positive
to ease the guilt of others.

Carol Casey
CANADA

A retired nurse, Carol has been nominated for the Pushcart Prize and has appeared in *The Prairie Journal, The Plum Tree Tavern, Sublunary, Grand Little Things, Bluepepper, The Anti-Langourous Project, Cacti Fur, Oyedrum, The Trouvaille Review, Stanza, Smokey Blue Literary and Arts, Spank the Carp, RAW Journal of Arts, Bindweed, Better than Starbucks, Amethyst Review, Assisi, The Ethicist, Neologism Poetry, Field Guide Poetry Magazine, Please See Me, Night Music Journal, Reapparition, Bureau of Complaint, Vita Brevis Press, Adanna, Cypress, Front Porch Review, Inscribe Journal, Faith Hope and Fiction, Eucalyptus and Rose, Minnow Literary, Blue Unicorn, The Lake, Hags on Fire, Sparks of Calliope, Whistling Shade, The Blotter, Poetic Sun, The Elevation Review, Lockdown Babybabble, Global Poemics, Euonia Review, Green Ink Poetry, The Brown Bag Review, The Mindful Word, Dust Magazine, The Pinyon Review, The Stickman Review, Three Line Poetry, Backchannel, Poetic Sun, Subterranean Blue, Poetry Village, Writers Resist, Walled Woman* and *Poetically*. She has contributed to a number of anthologies, most recently *Much Madness, Divinest Sense, Tending the Fire, i am what becomes of broken branch, We Are One: Poems from the Pandemic, Rearing in the Rearview - Quillkeepers Parenting Anthology, Beliveau Books Denouement Anthology, Blyline Legacies - An Anthology by Writers for Writers* - Cardigan Press.
E: ccasey@tcc.on.ca
W: www.learnforlifepotential.com/home-2/poetry/
FB: @caseypoetry
Twitter: @ccasey_carol

ODE TO THE EAST WIND

You come from where our stark beginnings find
their birth and blow through truth and storm to where
the roots of cold dig deep and make us blind
with tears that freeze on faces wild with care
and make escape from you such great relief
that other burdens seem so light to bear
when we are left with only human grief
to gather up within some sheltered lair
while you go on to taunt the naked trees
And howl your lonely dirges through the air
where sere fates toss about like brittle leaves
that sweep both nerve and landscape into prayer.
For it's your careless power we resist
and challenged, find the courage to persist.

First published in *Sparks of Calliope*, 2020.

TOADS AND MAIDENS

Don't assume, because some creature rests in your
palm, that they are safe as they know they're not.
Dry, rough, bumpy texture like braille, read the
message: *I'm better free. My biochemical language
is telling you something vital in the only way
I have: I want to be free. I can make you sick,
just set me down and wash your hands,
don't touch again.*

I wish I could give our daughters this power
to telegraph toxins to unwanted touch, leers, jeers
innuendos that eat away at, soil on, make a burden
out of walking down the street. No simple way to say
I'm better free. The rage can be toxin, or the pivot
that burns the brush, clears the detritus, takes a stand,
*leave me alone, wash your hands, unless invited,
don't touch again.*

First published in *Writers Resist*, 2020.

AFTER A NIGHT OF PAIN

My mind is still steaming
still dreaming of comfort.
My body's still burning
The world is still turning.
I greet the day drunken
from so little sleeping
my body still tight
from the echo of pain.
my muscles still bound
to the vigil they're keeping,
waiting like dry wood
to burst into flame.

I pray that this agony
has some mulch purpose.
I offer it up
like a blood sacrifice.
Let it burn karma
or lighten some burden
pay for admission
to some higher learning
where what matters most
is not what we think -
where I drink from its fountain,
soul widened and deepened
until cast, exhausted
on some peaceful shore.

Rose Menyon Heflin
WISCONSIN, USA

Originally from southern Kentucky, Rose is a poet and artist who loves travel and all aspects of the natural world. She majored in Environmental Studies and East Asian Languages and Cultures at Beloit College. Among other venues, her poetry has recently been published or is forthcoming in *50 Haikus, Ariel Chart, Asahi Haikuist Network, Bramble, The Closed Eye Open, The Daily Drunk, Deep South Magazine, Dreich Magazine, Eastern Structures, The Ekphrastic Review, Haikuniverse, Heartfelt Poetry Collection* (an anthology by Wingless Dreamer Publications), *The Light Ekphrastic, Littoral Magazine, Please See Me, Plum Tree Tavern*, *Poetry and Covid, Red Alder Review, Red Eft Review, Sparked Literary Magazine, The Texas Poetry Calendar, Three Line Poetry, Trouvaille Review, Visual Verse, The Wisconsin Poets' Calendar*, and *The Writers Club*. Her poetry recently won a Merit Award from Arts for All Wisconsin.
E: rosemenyonheflin@gmail.com

EVERYDAY HERO: A TANKA SEQUENCE

I.
Tender neurons twirl
As your heart rends into two
Another challenge
You are loathe to face
In a world raging with hate

II.
How to remain calm -
To dance out this latest storm?
When your feet are tired
Your mind and soul exhausted
Your body screaming its aches

III.
You may be winded
But you know that you will breathe
Freely once again
Despite all the obstacles
You always keep on living

IV.
Maybe it's hope,
Or perhaps mere stubbornness
That keeps you rising
After each blow you receive
You think it unimportant

V.
All that matters now
Is that you stagger upward
On your feet again
To take a couple more steps
To make a bit of progress

VI.
Colossal problems
So many centuries' worth
Rest on your shoulders
Delicate though they may seem
Beleaguered and wary

VII.
With warrior blood
A wise mind and astute eyes
A peacemakers' heart
You carry the torch proudly
So adept at surviving

VIII.
Knowing well life is hard
Yet still you keep on laughing
Smiling through the pain
Accomplished at finding joy
In every day's minutiae

IX.
Some will ignore you
Indifferent to your plight
Others will snub you
Thinking themselves much better
Still, some will offer pity

X.
But you do not quit
Screaming our troubles loudly
Until you are hoarse
Preaching to all who would hear
To all who desire the truth -

XI.
Talk of solutions
To all of these vast problems
We inherited
So very unwillingly
Like those who came before us

XII.
Refraining again,
"Our society is broken!
It must be fixed now,
Lest it crumble to nothing,
Taking us along with it!"

XIII.
You are active, too
Not only talking the talk

But walking the walk
Steep uphill climb that it is
Pausing to help others up

XIV.
Pausing to reflect
On just how far you have come
On your past success
On the path that lies ahead
On how far you have to go

XV.
So undiscouraged
You rededicate yourself
To affecting change
To the battle, to the climb
To overcoming still more

XVI.
So very proudly
You wear every battle scar
That this life inflicts
Your determination strong
When faced with adversity

Prafull Shiledar
INDIA

Prafull is an eminent Marathi language poet-translator from Central India, and Chief Editor of a well known Marathi literary journal *Yugvani*. He has three poetry collections in Marathi, and one in Hindi. Translations of his poems are published in many languages including Malayalam, Gujarati, Telugu, Manipuri, English, German, Slovak and Czech. He has read poetry in many national and international poetry festivals and literary events in India, Europe, USA and Dubai, and in 2013 he was invited for poetry reading in 11th Ars Poetica International Poetry Festival, Bratislava, Slovakia. Prafull has written short stories, book reviews, film appreciations, interviews, travelogue and criticism, and is the recipient of a number of awards for his poetry, as well as for his translations including Sahitya Akademi Award by National Academy of Letters, New Delhi.
E: shiledarprafull@gmail.com
FB:@prafull.shiledar

POET IN RIOT
English Translation by Santosh Bhoomkar

On a quiet lonely night
Low shouts of the beginning of a riot
Are heard from the middle of a city
Sprawled distantly

Slowly the shouts become distinct
Familiar voice of everyone since long
Can be recognized
That's full of absolutely strange excitement

After the riot begins
Every person runs away alone in great rush
And the mob humming like wild bees
Keeps following

In the hands of the mob
There are weapons
Like rusted swords and sticks
And sharp knives and country daggers in villages
Or anything up to AK 47 in a city

One by one the organs of lone person
Caught in the grip of the mob fall limp
Getting blood it suddenly wriggles
Like a bird about to fly

On the deep slope of terror
The tremulous hearts keep rolling

The rising tumult stops at my door
"Pull him out"
"Burn that bastard alive"
Such shouts begins for me
With that a herd of roaring fox
Pass trembling over me
From foot to head

I pull my legs close to my stomach
Close my fists tightly
Begins to collapse limitless deep
Scratching myself cut through and through

With abrupt bang on the glared floor

Someone from the mob
Holding at my neck
Help me to get up

Waves of the mob wrestle with my body

Ripping my skin off
The mob tries to search
The hereditary colour of my blood

Breaking the walls of the house
The mob sniffs in every brick of the house
To search the provincial scent of the soil

The mob peels off the skin even of my language
and tastes the accents

At last turning back
It searches for all the valuable things one by one in the house

Taking aim the mob smashes
The transparent glittering chandeliers
Preserved by me for so many years having innate pull

Trampling over the scattered pieces of glass
The mob begins to run once again
Leaving red impressions of bloody feet behind
For the generations to come

Lisa Molina
TEXAS, USA

Lisa has a Bachelor of Fine Arts in Theatre and English Education. While not binging on her new favourite writer's works, she can be found working with students with special needs, writing, singing, playing the piano, or marvelling at nature with her family. Her poetry can be found in several literary journals including *Beyond Words Magazine, Trouvaille Review, Ancient Paths Literary Journal, The Ekphrastic Review, Down in the Dirt, Sad Girls Club Literary Blog, Indolent Books, Silver Birch Poetry and Prose, Amethyst Review*, and soon to be featured in *Peeking Cat*.
E: lisabmolina@gmail.com
W: www.lisalitgeek.wordpress.com
Instagram: @lisabookgeek
Twitter: @lisabmolina1

WAITING FOR LIFE

I am still waiting

in the paediatric
cancer transplant
unit.

Ten days
and nights.
So far.

Will his body embrace
the donated cord
blood cells?

(As my womb once
embraced him as an
unborn child?)

Or reject them.
Refuse them.
Causing his death.

The children
on the other sides
of two walls

of our room
have whispered
their final breaths.

My child is still breathing.
Living a life
between deaths.

What is he dreaming?
Has he descended to the depths?
Lying in a dark womb cave?

Lazarus awaiting?

First published in *Amethyst Review*, 3 April 2021.

Aaron Pamei
INDIA

Aaron is a civil servant. His poems mostly deal with social and human conditions. His work has appeared in various journals and anthologies. He is also a keen runner and has participated in marathons and Ultras across various parts of the country.
E: aaronpamei68@gmail.com

THE REDSTONED TOWER

The redstoned tower just stands there
Mute. Unfeeling. Unmoved.
It will stand there till it dies,
Till the sands between the stones
Bleed to the ground and turn to mud
And the colossus becomes a pile of rubble.
For now it doesn't care for the rain or the sun;
It will neither hear nor cry,
But will stand with its shadow over the land.
Some say we will blow horns on its rampart,
Others say there's death and decay on its dark side.
As the battle rages 'tween the rabbit and the duck,
The wheels turn inexorably in the rut.
But the wind will blow and the rain will fall;
Ozymandias will be reclaimed by the sands
Of time, from whence it came.

Monica Manolachi
ROMANIA

Monica is a lecturer of English and Spanish at the University of Bucharest. As a poet, she has published three collections, *Joining the Dots* (PIM, 2016), *Fragaria's Stories to Magus Viridis* (Brumar, 2012) *and Roses* (Lumen, 2007), and her poems have been published in *The Blue Nib, Artemis Poetry, Culture Cult, Crevice, Contemporary Literary Horizon* and others. In 2018, she co-authored the bilingual poetry collection *Brasília* (PIM, 2018) with Scottish poet Neil Leadbeater. *Performative Identities in Contemporary Caribbean British Poetry* (2017), is part of her work as a researcher and literary critic. She has published numerous academic articles on contemporary poetry and prose including *Multiethnic resonances in Derek Walcott's poetry*, in *Ethnic Resonances in Performance, Literature, and Identity* (2019), and *December 1989 and the concept of revolution in the prose of Romanian women writers*, in the *Swedish Journal of Romanian Studies* (2020). Over the past 15 years, she has translated various types of poetry, as well as several classical and contemporary novels into Romanian. In September 2016, her *Antologie de poezie din Caraibe* was awarded the 'Dumitru Crăciun' Prize for Translation at the International Festival Titel Constantinescu, Râmnicu Sărat. Her most recent translation project is the anthology *Over Land, Over Sea: Poems for Those Seeking Refuge* (Five Leaves, 2015). As a cultural journalist, she has published articles in local literary magazines, and the bilingual collection of interviews *Table Talk* (PIM, 2018).
E: monicamanolachi@yahoo.com
FB: @monica.manolachi
Twitter: @MonicaManolachi

OUT OF WATER

There's no need to dive into subconscious depths.
Here you are: a colourful blown glass fish.

Ten-inch long, mouth open to send out an echo,
a perfect silhouette of submarine fragility and fear.

The first sight of you made me for ever stare!
Did you really like it on top of early TV sets?

Nobody can catch you and hold you beside their boat.
Strangest home decoration, what are you?

Fish, are you still alive? Can I touch you?
I wonder if you have your own bones or a tongue.

Immobile like a stranded creature on a beach,
I cover you with my net and begin to hum.

You, silent witness, worshipped and despised,
I wish you weren't so stiff and breakable.

Have you returned my thoughtful gaze?
No, it's just the lights, shifting in the room.

Unusual remnant of the Paratethys Sea,
I let you go back into the ocean of the future –

Reader, I've been talking to myself, forgive me.
Water is not my element anymore and miss it.

Maid Čorbić
BOSNIA AND HERZEGOVINA

Maid is 21 years-old and from Tuzla. In his spare time he writes poetry. He is a member of the WLFPH (World Literature Forum Peace and Humanity), and the editor of the portal *First Virtual Space Olympic*, led by Dijana Uherek Stevanović, which aims to connect poets around the world. Maid's poetry has also been published in anthologies and magazines worldwide including in: Chile, Spain, Ecuador, San Salvador, United Kingdom, Indonesia, India, Croatia and Serbia, as well as in printed anthologies including *Sea in the palm of your hand*, *Stories from Isolation*, *Kosovo Peony* and others. In 2020, he was named the poet of the year by the Indo-Universe group, which is also engaged in charity work around the world.
E: detrix233@gmail.com
FB: @xcelendge
Instagram: @zaglavlje

THE FAILURE OF THE WORLD

Surrounded by people drinking water from us
so no way to understand our anomalies
we are people eager for new developments around us
and we are looking for some solutions that are far away

We pack our strengths and weaknesses in one expensive gift
so we blame all the pigs on other people
just because our lives are no more luxurious than others
rather we live it miserable day after day

Our routines change over time steadily ours
and every thing in the world begins to lose its meaning
if we are human, we must love others around us
not to turn departure into cranial loss

And when one of us consciously leaves because of the situation
remember that you are never alone in the world
and that there is certainly reason to smile again
because there is someone who understands your problems

Our parents are our saviours for the misfortunes of the pig
there is no force that can stop us abruptly
interruption and tinnitus occur only then
when for a solution we turn a deaf ear in every sense

The world is unpredictable with a lot of adversity that we create them
ourselves
but so let us look forward to some better day of life
for no one is born to be in a world of silence and lying
and everyone will be equally responsible for all mistakes

People are that; the misfortunes of the world we meet every day
in the shaft of the player's eye is a fuse packed for the last time
for so much life is transience, that we do not see around us
that every misfortune is a creation of man's state of mind!

Alun Robert

ENGLAND

Born in Scotland of Irish lineage, Alun is a Kent based prolific creator of lyrical free verse achieving success in poetry competitions across the British Isles and North America. His work has been published by UK, Irish, European, African, Indian, US and Canadian literary magazines, anthologies and webzines. He is a member of the Mid Kent Stanza, the Rye Harbour Poetry group and the Federation of Writers Scotland for whom he was a Featured Writer in 2019.

BIRDSONG

Am perched behind bars
Door locked from the outside
Darkness arrives at nine under
A blanket of isolation.

Freedom so close by
But too far to exploit
Even when let out for an hour
When my cell is refreshed.

Fed twice a day or
When my head starts to bob
Fruit, vegetables, nuts, pellets
And on Sunday, fresh flowers.

But dandelions, chickweed
Hawthorn berries, rose hips
Wheat grass and legumes
Would be delicious in my diet.

While fresh water proffered
In steel cups (without saucers)
But never a single malt
Or bitter or strong cider.

And they call me Pretty Boy
Though not strictly correct
For that was long ago
After a visit to some vet.

Yet when a chance occurs
My repetition of cackles
In tones they recognise
To make them laugh and giggle.

Though there are no foes here
Apart from the Van and the Boa
Who come up to visit
With eye to eye contact.

At threatening times like those
Am grateful for jail

Safe from predators
With meal on their minds.

But soon after isolation
Door locked from the outside
Darkness arrives at nine then
Am perched on a bar.

TUO YAW

after clearance by a consultant
(he calls himself Mr)
entouraged by a troupe
like Rudi Nureyev,
I combine my chattels
into a dingy duffle bag
seen better days
just like moi,
to amble along beige corridors
by wards of the wounded
oozing a bouquet of disinfectant
smarting my senses,
passed the surplus on stretchers
with a tinge of incontinence
distraught after hours alone
waiting on a saline drip
then encounter Reception
of cheery smiles, frustrated
from staring at blank screens
(system down yet again)
when I look deep into a mirror
marled at the edges
swinging gently in the breeze
entering the exit
to find a fraction of my former self
and a neon light proclaiming
TUO YAW to greet me
en route to recovery,
through a process protracted
for healing will take its time
as I walk the tightrope twixt
bossa nova and au revoir

Suchismita Ghoshal
INDIA

Suchismita hails from West Bengal. With an academic career in science, she is currently pursuing her masters in business administration (MBA) from GD Goenka University in Gurgaon, Haryana. At just 23 years-old, Suchismita is also a professional multi-award winning writer, published author, internationally acclaimed poet, literary critic, literary influencer, content writing member for the West Bengal United Nations Youth Association, the International Organisation Of United Nations Volunteers, and the Helping Hand International Organisation. With more than 520 coveted co-authorship in various renowned national and international anthologies, prestigious literary magazines, websites, webzines and eminent literary journals and have been translated into Arabic and Italian. She has also authored three poetry books by the name of *Fields of Sonnet*, *Poetries in Quarantine* and *Emotions & Tantrums*.
E: ghoshalsuchismita019@gmail.com
W: www.suchismitaghoshal.com
FB: @suchismita.ghoshal.96,
Instagram: @storytellersuchismita
Wordpress: www.creativesuchi.wordpress.com

THE FAIRYTALE OF AUTUMN, IN THE KINGDOM OF NATURE

What an absolute pleasure it is
For my eyes to get a soothing therapy
When the leaves are yellowing, fading from
One colour to another and finally making its way
To slither away into the ground;
Like humbly setting a proud milestone
From the tender innocence of being a shoot,
Getting exposure as a green nubile leaf
And finally maturing towards the senility
To complete its own beautiful cycle of senescence.
The greenery envies me as well as enchants me
The way it unwraps the huge possibilities
Of adventure in every nook and corner
After getting exposed to the challenges of outer world, - the largest
field of possibilities after the ever-expanding skies;
I have seen the orangish glow when autumn arrives,
I have found myself wondered when I can't take
My eyes off from the spellbinding cotton like soft
Snowy clouds scattering here and there in
Separate clusters as if they are students coming
From different squads to have fun and gossip.
With Autumn, my Bengali soul is awakened
To that extreme level where nothing comes
Into the league of supremacy than of Durga puja.
The redolent smell of "Nyctanthes" fascinates me
With the euphoria of getting swayed away into the sanctity.
My imaginative heart knits a lot of stories
Where most of them are poured into the bowl of impassioned heart-
sap.
Bittersweet nostalgia outlines my fairytales
Of visiting autumn every year with some extravagant colours,
My feelings have overwhelming resemblance
With the ancient goddess, might have been
Embodying inside me, ageing slowly and Witnessing autumns and
celebrating
My birthdays through the gallops of the era.
The white spikes of catkin bewitch with its
Piousness of pendulous wandering in a queue Through the edges of
long rural roads.
The seasons oscillate in a cycle, forgiving
The tyrannies of concrete world,
While the most awaited revolution can break out

On a sudden autumn day prosecuting the evil minds.
Tumultuous revivification can easily be detected
Through the transformations of the most amiable Leaves through the
tiny cracks and discolouration
If we are vibrant enough to catch the signals!
Let us give ourselves the opportunity
To receive the utmost hospitality from the nurture of mother nature.
Night and day, words of sanctity will evolve
Into its finest version by curing me, you, us, all of us
And the whole world shall sing the hymn of nature and its seasons!

Dr. Achingliu Kamei
INDIA

Dr. Achingliu is a poet, a short story writer and an ultra-marathon runner. Her poetry has been published in several journals and in anthologies in India, USA, Singapore and Australia. She has a published book of poems, *Songs of Raengdailu*. She is currently living in Delhi.

E: achingliuk@gmail.com

SUMMER WAVES

Soft breeze flows in the open window,
On a calm morning,
The silence broken by a piercing siren,
The ambulance hurtling down the road,
Adding to the numbers
A mother, a father, a son, a daughter
In random order, no longer statistics
A friend, a face of a loved one.

Staring out the window, looking for a soul
Deserted roads, leading to no particular destination,
Searching for an oasis, a green patch for a choked lung
Last days of spring coming to an end,
Giving way to the summer waves
A lull after the first wave, then the second, third
In a horrific rush, bodies tumbling into pits,
Onto pyres, in a rush, pushed over the edge,
Not ready, dreams not fulfilled, no time to say goodbyes,
Denied of dignity in death.

***

The tsunami of disasters
Ushered in untold grief by the apathy of the ones,
Who should have been responsible?
Scurrying, scrambling with the dogs
For the ephemeral fame, to immortalize? a puny life.
Careful culling by the power, strategizing
Cultivating selfishness, materialism
In the garb of bringing development
Economy precedence take, self-glorification,
Leaving a path of destruction and death
In the quest to become a god.

THE PIED PIPER

No need to panic or be nervous.
Everything is in control.
The grim reaper proclaimed.

The violent knitting and weaving, lies told to masses.
Endorsed by his sycophants. You will not die.
You are safe in natural medicine.

The medicine-man made his millions
Now the sweet souls are all resting - eternally
The strategist swats at unwanted flies

Death visits all those who spoke
The great hero will make it brief for you -
Should you decamp- You chicken?

Mass produced. Blood will flow again. Applause.
Then the workers will be sent out again -
To the battlefield for the third time, the ones that survived.

As the pied piper polishes his next song,
His faithful clone just a shadow away -
Waiting for his thrill, his flagpole higher, flag bigger.

The muted orphans. His minions, dancing the death waltz
Master of the show, magic up his sleeve- lights, music
He sang his song, wove his magic, and the show is ready.

The factory will spin on, no stopping
Innocent souls, will they come back to tell the truth?
On the pied piper. Only time will tell.

THE LEH DRIVER

squinting into the dark
moon-washed nights
waves of memories
windshield, water strider.
tailing trucks through snow covered terrains
brake lights blinked ahead on the turns
as he chanted to himself and the snow
don't fall, don't slip
driving hard, hard life, strong faith
overtaking a truck ...
all the poems he ever sung
the ghazals for company
where life and death is real.
under a lonesome moon
eighty, slumped in a wheelchair,
grey hair , balding, sun tan gone ages ago
half-paralyzed, life in slow motion
he pauses, remembering, from forty years ago,
and calls out Spiti, Leh
having driven through the mountain
highs and lows of terrain and life
merge together in the warm autumn sun.
where am I?" he asked his son.
the son mentions the places he'd driven to
a moment, he seems to remember and smiles,
seeing himself on the precipice
driving his truck ...

Julie Ann Tabigne
SINGAPORE / PHILIPPINES

Julie Ann is a domestic worker from Philippines. She has worked in Singapore for eight years. She is a Team Leader of non-profit organization Uplifters, and a member of Migrant Writers of Singapore. E: jannesakura021115@gmail.com

SHADOW

Last five years was the darkest
It was messy
Living in the shadows of words
Scared to be judge
Incapability to fight for my own
Freedom never existed on that moment
Until such time I became tired
I need to regain my happiness
I need to do something
Crying is not helping me anymore

I stand up
It wasn't easy
Every morning I put a smile on my face
I've promised to be deaf
From everyone's perception
I listened to the music
that boosts my energy
I bought confidence
its expensive
But it's all worth it

Now, I must say that
I am so much happier
my heart is lighter
I forgive even they don't ask for it
It's the best thing I know
To start my whole life again
with so much positivity in me
I keep on moving,
Growing and continue improving.

Mary Anne Zammit

MALTA

Mary Anne is a graduate from the University of Malta in Social Work, in Probation Services, in Diplomatic Studies and has a Masters in Probation. She has also obtained a Diploma in Freelance and Feature Writing from the London School of Journalism. She is the author of four novels in Maltese, and two in English. Some of Mary Anne's literary works and poetry have also been featured in international magazines and anthologies and set to music and performed during the Mdina Cathedral Art Biennale in Malta. Also, her artistic works have been exhibited in various collective exhibitions both locally and abroad.

E: mariefrances3@gmail.com

THE WAY OUT

Obstacles are part of life
They always come as part of the game called life.
Adversity comes when least accepted.
I reach up for the skies.
Trying to get answers.
Maybe understand why.
It is part of the lesson.
Fighting a wind which comes.
Unwanted.
Unexpected.
But the skies always show the way.

Jenelyn Leyble
SINGAPORE / PHILIPPINES

Mother of two, Jenelyn is a Filipino domestic worker and caregiver to a stroke patient in Singapore. She has had a passion for writing since she was young. As part of Migrant Writers of Singapore, through literature, she helps others cope with life's challenges. Her poetry has been published in *Poetry Planet* and *Passion for Poetry*.
E: jenelynleyble@yahoo.com

I WILL RISE AND BLOOM

I feel helpless and devastated,
The moment you left,
There's no sunshine that brightens my day
No glimpse of smile upon my face

I'm alive though I feel breathless
I'm moving but half body buried,
I'm sleepy yet my eyes and mind wide awake
I'm hungry yet full of hesitations and worried

After I cry the whole night,
I promise myself I will rise and shine again,
You will see the brightest smile upon my face,
You see the bloomy look I used to be.

Like a flower in the desert I had to grow in the cruelest weather
Holding on to every drop of rain
Just to stay alive.

I've learned don't wait someone to bring you flowers. Plant your own
garden and decorate your own soul.
Where flowers bloom so does hope.

Hanh Chau

CALIFORNIA, USA

Born in Vietnam, of Chinese descent, Hanh has a Bachelor's and Master's degree in Business administration. During her spare time, she enjoys writing, listening to music and spending with her family.
E: hanhchau387@yahoo.com

A DELICATE FLOWER

Like a delicate flower
YES,
I endured through
Many battles of stormy weather
Day and night
rain and shine
And that I stayed strong
Like a delicate flower
I SURVIVED
Through many hardship
Of thirst quest and bitter cold
NEVER TO GIVE UP
Like a delicate flower I have never
relinquished my beauty title
I still stand tall
to carry my petals with
grace and poise
Like a delicate flower I have passed through
many capricious seasons to come
with the various change in life
Yet, I still hold myself up high
Like a delicate flower I was TOLD
As a fragile and vulnerable image portrayed
That I could NOT overcome my way
Above of all I have surpassed through many
Obstacles as it comes
That instilled with determination
To conquer of all
To grow into
A beautiful and enchanting display

Maria Editha Turingan Garma-Respicio
HONG KONG / PHILIPPINES

Maria's passion with writing started at age nine, and was active in the school paper. At age 14 she had a short story published in *Liwayway* magazine. She is a member Migrant Writers Of Hong Kong, Planet Poetry, and many other international writers groups, and has won various poetry competition both local and abroad. Maria has also has her poetry published in a number of anthologies including *Metaphors Of Life*. She holds a degree in Nursing, Physical Therapy, English Language Literature and Computer Science. She believes that writing is the best form of art, the best way to express one's self, and the best therapy ... ever.

E: garmaedith8@gmail.com
FB:@editha.g.respicio

ALL IS VANITY

In her youth, she had reached the peak of success, but it's fleeting,
gone so quick
Though she had millions in the bank
But she can't buy immortality
Or restore her lost dignity

Once she was the pride of youth
Now the burden to society

She's in the final curtain of her life now
Alone, her heart bleeds with sorrow
They all left when she needed them the most
They left behind futile granny-their native ancestry
Her pet is her lone companion in solitary

All alone, she's wallowing in self-pity
Who cares? She's now nonentity
Only her consort, kitty
Will weep when she will go to eternity

END

ADVERSITY, VOLUME 1 – FEATURING:

Phyliss Merion Shanken - NEW JERSEY, USA; Niels Hav – DENMARK; Ed Ahern - CONNECTICUT, USA; Kathy Sherban – CANADA; Michael Ceraolo - OHIO, USA; Ali Alhazmi - SAUDI ARABIA; Ndaba Sibanda - ZIMBABWE / ETHIOPIA; C.S. Kempling – CANADA; Michelle Morris – ENGLAND; P. J. Reed – ENGLAND; Nolo Segundo - NEW JERSEY, USA; Linda M. Crate - PENNSYLVANIA, USA; Fahredin Shehu – KOSOVO; Monsif Beroual – MOROCCO; Mark Andrew Heathcote – ENGLAND; Alicia Minjarez Ramírez – MEXICO; Gary Shulman - CALIFORNIA, USA; Mukund Gnanadesikan - CALIFORNIA, USA; Joralyn Fallera Mounsel - PHILIPPINES / SINGAPORE; John Grey - USA / AUSTRALIA; Nancy Shiffrin - CALIFORNIA, USA; Francis H. Powell – ENGLAND; Ana Stjelja – SERBIA; Lynn White – WALES; Germain Droogenbroodt - SPAIN / BELGIUM; Judy DeCroce - NEW YORK, USA; Antoni Ooto - NEW YORK, USA; Shikdar Mohammed Kibriah – BANGLADESH; Pavol Janik PhD – SLOVAKIA; Srđan Sekulić – SERBIA; Gayle Bell - TEXAS, USA; Tali Cohen Shabtai - ILLINOIS, USA; Ana M. Fores-Tamayo - CUBA / USA; Aminath Neena – MALDIVES; Bryan Andrews - SOUTH AFRICA; Borche Panov - REPUBLIC OF NORTH MACEDONIA; Daniela Andonovska-Trajkovska - REPUBLIC OF NORTH MACEDONIA; Karen Douglass - COLORADO, USA; Cordelia Hanemann - NORTH CAROLINA, USA; Zorica Bajin Đukanović – SERBIA; Joan McNerney - NEW YORK CITY, USA; Wansoo Kim PhD - SOUTH KOREA; Carl 'Papa' Palmer-WASHINGTON, USA; Caroline Johnson - ILLINOIS, USA; Alonzo "zO" Gross - PENNSYLVANIA, USA; Alisa Velaj – ALBANIA; Jyotirmaya Thakur - ENGLAND / INDIA; Fabrice Poussin - GEORGIA, USA; Patrick O'Shea - NETHERLANDS / UK; Russell Willis - VERMONT, USA; Paul S. Mugano – UGANDA; Michael Estabrook - MASSACHUSETTS, USA; Susan Sonde - MARYLAND, USA; Alexious J. Kachepa – MALAWI; Lou Faber - FLORIDA, USA; Eliza Segiet – POLAND; Mark Fleisher - NEW MEXICO, USA; Anthony Ward – ENGLAND; Mark J. Mitchell - CALIFORNIA, USA; Nelie Bautista - SINGAPORE / PHILIPPINES; Jack D. Harvey - NEW YORK, USA; Norbert Góra – POLAND; Tamam Kahn - CALIFORNIA, USA; Kristine Ventura - MALAYSIA / PHILIPPINES; Shweta Shanker - INDIA / SWITZERLAND; Igor Pop Trajkov - REPUBLIC OF NORTH MACEDONIA; Kevin Brown - ARKANSAS, USA; Ndumiso Maphumulo - SOUTH AFRICA; Pat Smekal – CANADA; Gary Beck - NEW YORK, USA; Carolyn Martin - OREGON, USA; Neil Leadbeater – SCOTLAND; Amrita Valan – INDIA; Rema Tabangcura - PHILIPPINES / SINGAPORE and Mantz Yorke – ENGLAND.

OTHER COLLECTIONS FROM THE POET

FRIENDS & FRIENDSHIP
With 248 contributions from 175 poets in 46 countries, and from 26 states in the US; published in two volumes, FRIENDS & FRIENDSHIP is our most contributed to anthology to date.
Vol. 1 – USA & CANADA – ISBN: 9798538022373
Vol. 2 - REST OF THE WORLD – ISBN: 9798538072590

FAITH
With 234 contributions from 151 poets in 36 countries, and from 30 states in the US; published in two volumes, FAITH is probably one of the largest and most significant international collections of poetry on the theme of faith ever published.
Vol. 1 - USA – ISBN: 9798740844695
Vol. 2 - REST OF THE WORLD – ISBN: 9798740924557

CHILDHOOD
With over 300 contributions from 152 poets in 33 countries worldwide, and across 28 States in the USA, CHILDHOOD is in two volumes and is our most popular collection to date.
Vol. 1 - USA - ISBN: 9798564862332
Vol. 2 – REST OF THE WORLD - ISBN: 9798593564696

CHRISTMAS
With over 150 contributions from 97 poets in 34 countries, CHRISTMAS is probably one of the largest international anthologies of Christmas poetry ever published.
153 poems / 275 pages.
ISBN: 9798564859837

A NEW WORLD - Rethinking our lives post-pandemic.
Sixty-seven poets from around the world all writing on the theme of A NEW WORLD, exploring life post-pandemic.
115 poems/225 pages
ISBN: 9798696477084

ON THE ROAD Volumes 1 & 2
With 120 poets from around the world, ON THE ROAD, is probably one of the largest international anthologies of travel poetry ever published.
Vol. 1: ISBN: 9798640673593
Vol. 2: ISBN: 9798665956312

WAR & BATTLE
Fifty-four poets from around the world all writing on the theme of WAR & BATTLE.
103 poems/215 pages.
ISBN: 9798629604594

THE SEASONS
Thirty-four poets from around the world all writing on the theme of THE SEASONS.
80 poems/129 pages.
ISBN: 9798600084445

LOVE
THE POET's very first collection. Twenty-nine poets from around the world all writing on the theme of LOVE.
73 poems/119 pages.
ISBN: 9781699169612

Printed in Great Britain
by Amazon